MURDER & MAYHEM
IN
WASHTENAW COUNTY

MURDER & MAYHEM
— IN —
WASHTENAW COUNTY

James Thomas Mann

THE
History
PRESS

Published by The History Press
Charleston, SC
www.historypress.com

Copyright © 2022 by James Thomas Mann
All rights reserved

First published 2022

Manufactured in the United States

ISBN 9781467151757

Library of Congress Control Number: 2022939457

CONTENTS

PREFACE

Washtenaw County, Michigan, has, throughout its history, been fortunate to have a consistently low level of crime. These crimes—for the most part, robbery, burglary, shoplifting and so on—are traumatic for the victims but leave the rest of the community untouched. Every now and then, however, a crime sends shockwaves through the county and beyond.

Murder, the taking of a human life by another, is the ultimate crime, as it denies the victim whatever potential they may have had. Whatever that person may have done or may have become is lost forever. This is the crime of murder.

This is perhaps why murder holds such fascination, as it brings about an unchangeable end. The one who is left dead is not the only victim of a murder, as the crime sends out a shockwave through an ever-expanding circle of family and friends. They suffer a sense of loss that can never be fully overcome, as well as guilt, the question they ask of themselves of could they have prevented the crime? There is also the guilt of words unspoken or unheard and of things left undone—the things that cannot be. Feelings such as these can send the soul of those who remain alive into the darkness of depression.

Sometimes, out of the darkness of such a depression can come redemption and the possibility to understand, forgive and find peace. Where there is understanding and forgiveness, there is hope for humanity.

The following are fifteen stories of murder and mayhem from the history of Washtenaw County. There is pain, loss and, at times, mercy.

ACKNOWLEDGEMENTS

I wish to say thank you to all those who helped make this book possible. I am grateful for all the help I received from Kathy Ziegler, who read each chapter and corrected my typos and misspellings and pointed out what needed work and clarification. She also made useful suggestions on how to improve the work. The look of the book was improved by Rebecca Murphy, who scanned most of the images in the book. Additional scanning was done by Al Rudisill. Darla Welshons, a librarian at the Ann Arbor District Library, scanned all the stories of the Kristine Kutz murder published by the *Ann Arbor News* and placed them online. Because of the help I received, this is a better book than I could have produced alone.

1

A TERRIBLE AFFAIR AT LYNDON

THE MURDER OF MARTIN BREITENBACH

On the afternoon of Saturday, August 2, 1873, eight young men and boys from Scio Township went to Lyndon Township to pick whortleberries. They started picking the berries in a swamp on the property of John Cassidy, who ordered them off of his land. Cassidy told the young men that the swamp was sacred to him, as were his orchard and the rest of his farm. The young men did not leave; instead, they snatched his cane from him and used it to beat him. They struck him over the head with the cane several times. When they were done, the young men left him.

The young men then went to another part of the swamp that belonged to Martin Breitenbach. There, some young women and girls were picking berries. The young men treated the young women to what was described as "a profusion of oaths, obscene talk and vile epithets." The young women left the swamp and went to Breitenbach, a farmer of about fifty years of age who was plowing a nearby field.

Breitenbach went to the road bordering the swamp and ordered the young men to leave. The young men refused to go. At this, Breitenbach fired a gun he had, aiming over the heads of the young men. Then the young men moved toward Breitenbach, swearing and cursing at him for having a gun. Six of them had sticks in their hands, and one, Edward H. Bycraft, carried a stone in each hand. The young men took hold of Breitenbach, some by his clothes, and two grabbed his gun. The gun was taken from Breitenbach, and one of the men struck him with a stone from behind on the right side of his head. The blow to Breitenbach's head knocked him off the road, and he lay on the ground for three minutes.

Breitenbach got up and stepped back onto the road. He spoke and reached into his pocket.

Someone exclaimed, "He has a pistol!"

They took hold of his arms and found he had been reaching for his pipe.

Someone said, "Let him have it."

A neighbor named Hugh Cassidy, who was over eighty years of age, told the young men that they better leave. And they did, several of them dropping stones as they turned away.

Breitenbach went to his house and then to his field, where he resumed plowing. He managed to plow twice around the field before he was seen falling on his face, as if in a faint. He was carried to his house, and a doctor was sent for. He never regained consciousness and died at about 7:00 p.m. on Sunday. A postmortem examination held on Monday found that his skull had been badly fractured. Breitenbach left a wife and eleven children behind.

That same day, a warrant was issued for the arrest of the eight young men and boys, Edward H. Bycraft, George Bycraft, Walter Metcalf, George Metcalf, Henry Marsh, Elisha Marsh, Even Marsh and Ezra Marsh. Washtenaw County sheriff Fleming and his deputies were so prompt in their arrests of the eight young men that they did not know Breitenbach had died until after they were lodged in the jail at Ann Arbor.

Indictments were filed against the eight, but nolle prosequi was entered for George Bycraft and George Metcalf. The other six stood trial in November 1873 and were found guilty. The jury recommended the mercy of the court, and five of the six were given a small fine. Ezra Marsh was sentenced to one year in the penitentiary.

MURDERED IN HIS OWN BED

THE DEATH OF LUDWIG MILLER

A rumor is perhaps the one thing that can travel faster than the speed of light. Seemingly from nowhere, a story spreads far and wide, and as it travels, the facts change, and different people hear different versions of the same event.

This is what happened in the early hours of the morning on August 11, 1875, when news reached Ann Arbor that a farmer had been murdered while they were asleep. According to one version, burglars had broken into the house and killed the farmer to escape detection. Another version of the story said a number of men had surrounded the house and called the farmer out, and when he came to the door, they shot him. A third account of the crime said the farmer was murdered in his bed while he was asleep beside his wife.

At daylight, it was discovered that the murdered man was Ludwig G. Miller, a wealthy German farmer living in the Township of Scio, about seven miles west of Ann Arbor. Someone who knew the facts of the case, as they were then known, arrived at Ann Arbor at around 8:00 a.m. and said Miller had been shot by George Burkhardt, a nephew of Miller's wife. At this, Sheriff Fleming, Deputy Sheriff McIntyre, prosecuting attorney Frazer, Coroner Kapp and Dr. Frothingham, as well as a number of others, left for the scene of the crime.

At the farmhouse, Coroner Kapp held an inquest, and the facts of the matter began to come out. Frederika Miller, the wife of Ludwig, was awakened by something but did not know what just before midnight. She noticed that her husband's shirt was on fire. Once she had put out the fire, she noticed her husband's unnatural breathing. At first, she thought her husband had been struck by lightning. Then she called for Leonard Gehrenger, the couple's hired man, to come help her. The two carried Ludwig to a room on the other side of the house. There, they discovered he had been shot.

Frederika Miller went upstairs to look for George Burkhardt, who slept in the same room as Gehrenger. In the darkness, she felt Burkardt's bed and discovered he was not there. She then sent Gehrenger to the nearby farm of Jacob Jedele. George Burkhardt came into the room after Gehrenger had left. He ran around the room confusedly and cried.

At the inquest, Dr. Frothingham testified on his findings, having completed a postmortem examination of the body.

> *Found his rigor mortis well marked. Found a wound on the left shoulder near the apex, three-fourth of an inch in diameter. Outer edge ragged and sharply cut. Cuticle burnt off two inches in diameter. The inner side of the neck covered with smut; an appearance of carbon followed the wound from the opening to between the second and third ribs five inches from the backbone. The left lung was collapsed, and the whole cavity was filled with clotted blood. There were about three quarts of blood. The wound passed through the upper and lower lobes of the left lung, fracturing the seventh and eighth ribs. Ten in all. Found a piece of wadding in the wound. Heart and lungs healthy. One receiving such a wound would, in all, probably not be able to speak afterward.*

During the inquest, a reporter for the *Peninsular Courier* arrived and made his presence known, and after viewing the body, he asked if the murderer could be seen. He was surprised when a small boy dressed only in pants and a shirt was pointed out to him. This was George Burkhardt, who the reporter was told he could interview.

"What is your name?"

"George Burkhardt."

"How old are you?"

"I was fifteen years old on the tenth day of February."

"Don't you think this is a terrible affair?"

"It is awful."

The reporter could see he knew more about the murder than he said. The reporter asked him if he would tell him about the murder.

"What do you want to know for?"

The reporter told him no harm would come to him and asked if he would go up to his room and tell him how the murder was committed. Burkhardt seemed glad to get away from the crowd and went upstairs with the reporter.

The first question asked by the reporter was: "Did you murder Miller?"

Burkhardt smiled and said, "I shot him. I went to bed on Tuesday night but did not sleep much. After the folks were all in bed and asleep, I got up, went downstairs, got the double-barreled gun and went to his room. He lay high up on the pillow, and Mrs. Miller was low down in the bed. The baby was in the crib by the side of the bed."

Then, with a devilish smile on his face, Burkhardt raised his arms as if holding the gun. He said, "I shot him so!"

Burkhardt said Miller was lying on his right side, so Burkhardt held the gun over Mrs. Miller's head, about two feet from Ludwig's breast, and fired. Miller never stirred.

> *After I shot, I left the room and went into the sitting room. There was a light in the kitchen off the bedroom. I remained in the sitting room until I saw Mrs. Miller get up. She did not wake up right away after I shot. When I saw her, I went back upstairs in my own room and went to bed. The hired man slept in the same room with me but did not hear me when I went down or when I came back. I didn't think any person in the house heard the gun go off. Mrs. Miller called the hired man, and I was asleep. When I got up, I heard them say Miller was struck by lightning.*

Burkhardt was asked what his motive was for the crime.

"A short time since," answered Burkhardt, "Miller called me early in the morning, after which I laid down again and went to sleep, when Miller came up and whipped me. Since that, I have been mad at him. I first thought about shooting him on Tuesday. I would never do such a thing again."

Those who heard Burkhardt confess to the murder of Miller were sworn in and testified to hearing the confession, and at this, the jury of the inquest retired and returned a verdict: Ludwig Miller had come to his death on the night of August 10, 1875, from a gunshot received at the hands of George Burkhardt.

The sheriff asked Burkhardt if he had any boots. In answer, Burkhardt went to a corner of the room and picked up a nice pair of boots. Walking back to the sheriff, Burkhardt said, "These are my Sunday boots." The sheriff told Burkhardt to put the boots on, which he did. Then Burkhardt put on a neat gray suit, which Burkhardt called his "Sunday clothes." Once this was done, the sheriff pulled from his pocket a pair of handcuffs and put them on Burkhardt. His hands cuffed before him, Burkhardt looked behind him, as if to ask if he should take his old clothes with him. His clothes were gathered up and placed over his arms to cover the handcuffs from sight.

Then the undertaker announced that he had finished laying out the body of Miller, and all who wished to view the remains could do so. A large number of those present did so. Burkhart was taken into the room to view the body, and with a half smile on his face, he gazed at the remains. Then he was led out of the house, through the crowd, and taken to the jail at Ann Arbor.

After the crowd had passed by the body, the wife and five-year-old son of Miller entered the room. The wife kissed her dead husband and stroked his hair. Their son sobbed and called on his father to "Tiss me papa."

Every account of the murder states that Ludwig Miller treated George Burkhardt as if he were his own son. The accounts note that Burkhardt was taken in by Miller because his mother was unable to care for him and his brother. The accounts note that Burkhardt's father was killed during the Civil War, although he later referred to his father as if he was still alive. Yet it is likely that Miller saw Burkhardt not as a relative but as more of a source of cheap labor, treating him little better than an enslaved person.

That afternoon, Burkhardt was taken before Justice Beahan and pleaded guilty to the charge of murdering Ludwig Miller. He was then sent back to the jail to await trial at the next term of the circuit court.

On the Friday after the murder, Burkhardt was told by some of the other prisoners that Friday was hanging day, and as Burkhardt had committed a terrible crime, he was told he would hang that day. Burckhardt said it was as good as any day to hang. Burkhardt said he would rather be in jail than at work on the farm, as he got no fat pork to eat and no hard work to perform at the jail.

Burkhardt was taken to the circuit court on Tuesday, September 22, 1875, for trial. A number of witnesses were called to testify, but no new information was forthcoming. The judge called Burkhardt to come forward and answer his questions.

I am fifteen years of age; my father is in Saginaw, blacksmithing; my mother is not alive; don't remember her; I have lived with Miller seven years; was mad at him about a week before I shot him; made up my mind to kill him two days before and kept it in my mind all the time; Miller was kind to me the first few years I lived with him; I went to school a little last winter;

*got confirmed in church last winter; can write a little; have nothing to say
why sentence should not be pronounced.*

The judge gave Buckhardt some words of advice and then said: "Your
sentence is solitary confinement and hard labor in the state prison at Jackson
during your natural life. May God have mercy on your soul."

As Burkhardt was being taken back to the jail, the sheriff asked him what
he thought of the prospect before him. Burkhardt said it looked bad, but if
he was good, he would probably be pardoned in twenty-five or thirty years.

Burkhardt was pardoned by the governor in 1892.

3

MURDER AT DEXTER

L ate in 1877, William H. Morrand, a tall, powerfully built Black man about thirty years of age, arrived at the village of Dexter. Morrand asked permission of a Mr. Cullonine to erect a hut in the woods at the rear of his farm and near the tracks of the Michigan Central Railroad. Once permission was granted, Morrand set to work. The *Ann Arbor Courier* reported on Friday, January 25, 1878:

> *He excavated a foundation on a side hill in circular form, brought the boughs of some saplings together, then with old railroad ties and other rubbish fixed it so that he covered it over with earth; improvised a stove from old sheet iron and tin, collected some crude cooking utensils, and with crossed sticks and short saplings across and boughs and moss on top, set up housekeeping all alone and as secluded from the haunts of men as possible.*

Morrand went around to the farms and businesses of the area, asking for the things he needed. No one ever accused him of theft. Soon, he was an object of curiosity. Certain boys of the village got into the habit of visiting his hut to tease him and provoke his eccentricities. These boys treated him with cruelty, scattering his stores when he was away. The boys asked Mr. Cullonine for permission to cut down a tree so that it would fall on Morrand's hut and crush it. Mr. Cullonine refused to give his permission for any such act.

At about 10:00 a.m. on Sunday, January 20, 1878, eight boys and young men, Stephen Cavanaugh, Thomas McLaughlin, Thomas Fawley, Edward Conklin, Charles McGovern, William Sloan, Thomas Sloan and Dan Cunningham, started making their way to the hut of Morrand. They were accompanied by Thomas O'Grady, who was about thirty years of age.

Once they were at the hut, the boys began teasing Morrand, one even placing a log against the door of the hut as O'Grady fired a shot at a tree with his revolver. Morrand came out of the hut, holding an axe in his hands, and walked up to Stephen Cavanaugh and said, "I want you to leave." Cavanaugh asked Morrand not to strike him with the axe. At this, Morrand raised his axe and struck Cavanaugh with it, cutting his arm.

Standing nearby was O'Grady, who said to Cavanaugh, "If he strikes you again, I'll fix him."

Then Morrand made a rush at O'Grady. As Morrand approached, O'Grady told him to stand back. Then O'Grady fired another shot with his revolver. Morrand struck O'Grady on the head with the axe. As O'Grady ran backward, Morrand followed. Once again, Morrand struck O'Grady with the axe, and O'Grady fell to his knees. The eight others then started to run away. As they turned to run, O'Grady cried out, "For God's sake, boys, don't leave me." Morrand struck O'Grady a last and fatal blow with the axe.

Word of the death of O'Grady quickly spread, and officers were on their way to the hut when Morrand walked up to them and gave himself up. Dr. Alex Rogers arrived at the hut around 12:30 that afternoon and found O'Grady lying on the front of his body with the left side of his head up. Dr. Rogers found O'Grady's orbit bone smashed in and the bones of his nose broken. Between the two, Dr. Rogers found a depressed fracture in the skull that was large enough to admit three fingers.

That evening, the officers, thinking violence might befall Morrand, removed him to the jail at Ann Arbor. At the jail, the prosecuting attorney questioned Morrand and concluded he was insane. Morrand was sent to the asylum in Kalamazoo.

4

THE LINSLEY SHOOTING IN BRIDGEWATER

David R. Linsley was a farmer in Bridgewater Township who was known to be a hard drinker. His wife had left him, and she lived with their daughter in Ann Arbor. Sometime in early 1889, Linsley fell down the steps of his barn and hurt his shoulder. After this, he continuously wore an overcoat, even sleeping in it through the night on a lounge.

To help him work the farm of fifty acres, Linsley asked his son, also named David Linsley, and his son's wife, Minnie, to come to the farm and keep the house for him. David knew the pain in his father's shoulder must have been great for him to ask this of his son, as the two had always been quarrelsome. The trouble between the two men resumed after the son and daughter-in-law moved in. At one point, the father took a revolver out of his wardrobe and showed it to the son. The father told the son that if he ever touched him again, he would shoot him.

On the afternoon of Saturday, April 13, 1889, the father and son went to Bridgewater Station, a four corners community not far from the farm where there was a grocery. At the grocery store, the two drank beer freely. On their return trip home, a flock of wild ducks flew over their heads. Young Linsley took the revolver from his father's overcoat pocket to fire at the ducks.

Soon after the two returned home, they got into a discussion over some trifling matter while they were in the living room of the house. This discussion quickly turned into a quarrel. For some reason, the two men went from the living room and into the woodshed. There, the father would later say, the son picked up the handle of a mop. The son then struck the

STORE & RES. BRIDGEWATER STATION,
BY HENRY. GUTHARDT & SONS.

Bridgewater Station, where David Linsley and his son David R. Linsley stopped to drink before returning home. *From* Combination Atlas Map of Washtenaw County, Michigan.

father in the face with the mop handle. After the blow, the two clinched, and the son reached around and pulled the revolver out of his father's overcoat pocket. The father saw the revolver and seized it. As the two struggled for possession of the revolver, it discharged twice, one of the shots hitting the young Linsley.

Minnie, the wife of the young Linsley, had witnessed the quarrel start in the living room of the house but did not follow the two to the woodshed. When she heard the first shot, she started for the woodshed and heard the second shot before reaching the shed. When she entered the woodshed, she saw that her husband had hold of the revolver. His father may have had a grip on the gun as well, but she later said that she was not sure of this. Minnie took hold of the gun and asked her husband to let her have it. Her husband let go of the gun as she had asked. His father then left the woodshed and went toward the barn. The son followed his father until he stepped through the door; then he turned to one side, took a few steps and fell, exclaiming, "I am shot." Minnie went to her husband, who asked her where his father was. She told him his father had gone to the barn. To this, he said, "Call him; I am dying."

Minnie called the father, who went to get a dipper of water. He gave the dipper to Minnie and then turned to go to the barn. Again, the son asked where his father was and said that he should be called. The father was again called, and this time, he went to the spot where his son was lying. The son turned to his father and said, "You have killed your last son." To this, the father said nothing, but with the help of Minnie, he carried the son to the house and placed him on the lounge. Then the father turned away and left the house. The son died almost immediately after this.

After the shooting, a doctor was summoned, as was an officer. The father placed himself in the charge of the officer immediately after the shooting. A coroner's jury was formed, and Justice Myron Webb of Saline heard the testimony.

"The pistol used is a .32-caliber," reported the *Detroit Free Press* of Tuesday, April 16, 1889.

> *The ball entered the abdomen on a line with the navel and about five inches to the right, taking a downward course. At the postmortem examination, the ball could not be found. The pistol was discharged twice. The ball from the first or second discharge struck a churn, standing in the woodshed, about six inches from the floor, showing that when this discharge was made, the pistol pointed downward.*

The jury rendered a verdict, as reported by the *Ann Arbor Argus* on Friday, April 19, 1889: "That David R. Linsley came to his death from a pistol-shot wound, but whether the pistol was in the hands of his father at the time the fatal discharge, the jury were unable to decide."

On Monday April 15, 1889, prosecuting attorney Lehman and Deputy Sheriff Brenner went to Bridgewater to investigate the case. As this was the day of the funeral, they decided not to arrest Linsley at this time. Linsley agreed to go Ann Arbor the next day with his attorney and his son's widow.

Linsley arrived at Ann Arbor, as agreed, on Tuesday, April 16, 1889, with Minnie and Frank Jones, an attorney from Saline. After taking a statement from Minnie, Lehman decided to arrest Linsley for the killing of his son. A warrant was issued by Justice Pond, and Linsley was arrested and placed in jail. The examination was held before Justice Pond on Thursday, April 18, 1889. Linsley was bound over to the next term of the circuit court.

"Mr. Linsley is of medium height," reported the *Ann Arbor Courier* on Wednesday, April 17, 1889, "black hair, dark complexion, with a face bronzed by outdoor labor evidently. His face looks as if he had gone through quite a tussle, as his eyes are black and blue, and he has evidently been subjected to hard usage."

"The prisoner is pounded and scarred badly about the face," noted the *Ann Arbor Argus*, "the result of being struck with the mop in the melee."

Judge Kinne admitted Linsley with a $4,000 bail. His bail was provided by George Osborne of Saline and Linsley's ex-wife.

Nothing more was reported on the case until October 4, 1889, when the *Ann Arbor Argus* published a report on the term of the circuit court that was then concluding. "The criminal calendar is about all disposed of," noted the *Argus*. "The case of David Linsley for murder has been dropped, defendant giving a bond to keep the peace."

5

BANK ROBBERY AT DEXTER

On the morning of Thursday, March 1, 1894, H. Wirt Newkirk, a cashier at the Dexter Savings Bank, arrived at the bank around 8:00 a.m. The bank was a two-story brick building facing west on the main street of the village of Dexter. Every day, it seemed, half of the population of the village passed through its doors. As Newkirk entered the bank, he picked up the morning newspaper, which had been slipped under the door. After about five minutes, he set the paper down and stepped over to the vault. There, he found the doors to the vault unlocked. This did not surprise him, as Orla C. Gregory, the assistant cashier, knew the combination and sometimes unlocked the doors before the bank opened at 8:00 a.m.

Opening the doors to the vault, Newkirk was surprised to find Gregory lying on the floor, unconscious, and silver coins scattered around. Newkirk thought Gregory had had a fit and had fallen to the floor, scattering the coins from a tray. Newkirk rushed to his side and tried to revive him. After about five minutes, Gregory regained consciousness and told Newkirk a story worthy of the Wild West.

Gregory told Newkirk he had arrived at the bank at his usual time of 7:30 a.m. and opened the large front doors of the bank. Everything seemed normal; he did not notice any strangers on the street or have any cause for concern. He removed the ashes from the stove and emptied them in the yard behind the bank. Then he swept the floor and emptied the sweepings in the yard. Then he went back onto the bank. He later said:

The Dexter Savings Bank building as it appeared at the time of the robbery. *Used with the permission of the Bentley Historical Library, University of Michigan; from the Sam Sturgis collection, box no. 5.*

I remember when I went out that I heard the door click. I thought it was the boy who peddles the News *who comes in about that time….I just got back in the office when,* flash, *two pistols were thrust in my face. I was badly frightened, but I thought the time lock would save the cash. The men were masked, and one was shorter than the other, but both were rather short. They wore overcoats—I think they wore overcoats. I was badly scared, as you may suppose. They told me to open up if I valued me life, and I did open the vault.*

The safe in the vault was furnished with a timer that was set to run for twelve hours. The night before, the time lock was set at 7:30 p.m. and had just run down when Gregory opened the doors for the robbers. One of the robbers held Gregory while the other stuffed all the cash in the safe into his pockets. The robbers also carried away three sacks of silver weighing eighteen pounds.

Once the robbers had taken all the money, they started to walk out. Gregory followed them. The robbers then turned and struck Gregory on the head around his temple with either a stone or a sandbag. Then the robbers carried Gregory into the vault and closed the doors but did not lock them. The next thing Gregory knew, Newkirk was leaning over him to revive him.

A doctor was summoned, and Gregory was sent home. The authorities were notified, and every man who had a gun went in search of the robbers. Just about every outhouse and barn in Dexter was searched, but no trace of the men was found.

The *Washtenaw Evening Times*, on Thursday, March 1, 1894, noted:

No strangers had been seen to come into or leave the village, and consequently, a general air of mystery surrounds the entire affair. It is thought that the men must have had a horse and buggy close by, as otherwise, they would hardly have taken 18 or 20 pounds of silver with them. It was found that three men had got on the train going east this morning, but it is not thought that they were the men.

The *Evening News* reported on Friday, March 2, 1894:

One clue that seems to have some pertinence came to light last night. Two strangers were seen promenading in front of the residence of J. V.N. Gregory about 5 o'clock in the morning. Mr. Gregory is the father of the assistant

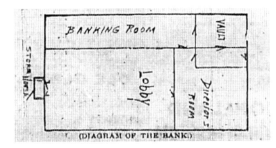

O. C. Gregory

Above: The layout of the interior of the Dexter Savings Bank. *From the* Detroit Evening News, *Thursday, March 1, 1894.*

Right: Orla C. Gregory, who was found on the floor of the bank after the robbery. *From the* Detroit Evening News, *Friday, March 2, 1894.*

cashier, who lives in another part of town, but it is supposed that the strangers confused the two and were waiting for young Gregory to go to his duties. These men were seen by two different residents of the village and were strangers to both.

The officers are working on the clue of a carriage that was seen about 7:45, standing on the street that joins the alley in the rear of the bank. Deputy Sheriffs George Bell of Dexter and M.C. Peterson of Ann Arbor are working on the case, and to the former gentleman, the News *is indebted for much valuable information. Mrs. Durns, who lives on the street back of the bank at the corner of the alley, says she saw a carriage in the street in front of her house at 7:45 a.m. "There was a man in the carriage, holding by the lines a bay horse. It was a top carriage, and the man wore a light overcoat and black cap. I did not see him drive away."*

M. Cummings, who lives a block further east, saw a rig answering the same description about the same time and place. He saw it start away but did not notice anyone get in and did not pay much attention.

Mrs. Quinn lives on the same street three blocks east. She saw the same rig drive by her house about the same time and kept right on east. Mrs. Chas. Trumbull, who lives on the corner of the alleyway and on the same street, says she saw a horse and buggy tied to a maple tree across the street opposite her home. The horse was light sorrel with top buggy. Two men came and got in about 7:45. Both wore dark overcoats; one wore a stiff derby hat, the other a slouch. They had no beards. They drove east very deliberately.

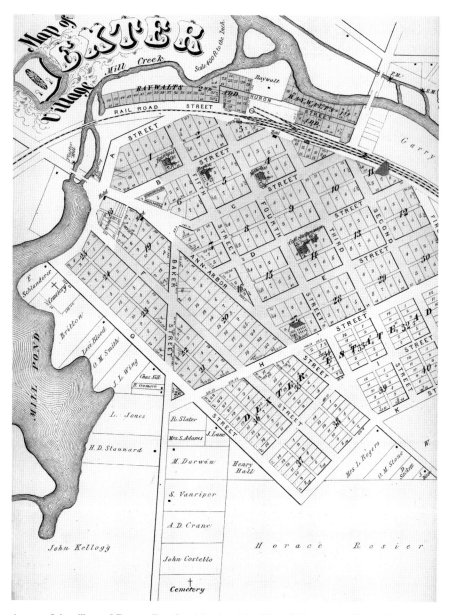

A map of the village of Dexter. *From* Combination Atlas Map of Washtenaw County, Michigan.

The *Washtenaw Evening Times*, on Wednesday, March 2, 1894, noted that there were no new developments in the case. The account further noted that the robbers were either remarkably lucky or well-informed. The robbers came when Gregory was alone in the bank and just when the time lock on the safe ran out.

> The facts would seem to lead to the suspicion that the robbers had a confederate in the village who posted them, but the general opinion is that no one in Dexter possesses the requisite nerve for such a deal and that it was carried out by professionals.
>
> The most remarkable part of the whole affair is that although there were people coming and going on the street, no one saw any strangers in the town or saw anyone enter or leave the bank, although it is about the most conspicuous building on the street. One man says he was back and forth in the alley behind the bank several times between 7 o'clock and 8 o'clock and saw nothing of anyone, nor did he see any horse and buggy or other rig about the place.

The deputy sheriffs who were leading the investigation had no clues, but they did have a suspect: Orla C. Gregory. The deputy sheriffs reasoned that the crime had to have been committed by someone who lived in Dexter, as no stranger had been seen near the bank at the time of the robbery. Gregory was clearly someone they wanted to talk to. After the discovery of the robbery, Gregory had been sent home, where he had stayed, seemingly too unnerved to be questioned. The deputies wanted to arrest Gregory, but the president and directors of the bank would not hear of such a thing. They refused to believe that Gregory had anything to do with the robbery. He was from a prominent family and was considered a fine, outstanding young man.

Finally, on Tuesday, March 6, 1894, Deputy Peterson talked a vice-president of the bank to agree to call in a detective from the Detroit Police Department to see if he would be of the same opinion as Peterson and the other deputies. That evening, Detective Alonzo Baker of the Detroit Police Department arrived in Dexter. Detective Baker began working on the case at seven o'clock the next morning.

Detective Baker began by familiarizing himself with the details of the case. He talked with the Chief Cashier Newkirk and had him point out the exact location where he had found Gregory. From Newkirk, Baker learned the time lock had been set the night before to open at nine minutes before

8:00 a.m. instead of at 8:00 a.m. sharp. This would have given the robberies only twelve minutes to commit the crime.

Baker talked with one of the men who aided Newkirk in reviving Gregory. The man told Baker that the back door of the bank was locked when he arrived. This proved the robbers could not have left the bank, as both doors were fastened from the inside.

Around noon that day, Baker searched the office at the rear of the vault. In the room was a washstand. Baker was told the washstand was stationary, so he pulled it from the wall. There, he found two bags of money. One bag contained $312.55 in gold coin and the other $638.75 in silver coin. Then Baker asked that Gregory be sent for. Gregory was summoned but told he was wanted at the bank to look over the books. At the bank Gregory was asked if he could remember more details of the robbery. Gregory said he could not add anything to what he had said before. Then Baker showed him the two bags of coin. At the sight of the bags, Gregory turned pale and nearly fell to the floor. He did not speak for nearly ten minutes; then, with a gasp, he exclaimed, "I did it myself!"

Under questioning by Baker, Gregory revealed where the rest of the money was hidden. Baker went to the Gregory house and found a roll of $1,500 in the pocket of a coat and $1,000 in a drawer. Gregory told Baker that he had contemplated the robbery since the previous Monday and carried out the plan just before Newkirk had arrived. He had struck his head against the wall of the vault to produce the bruise he claimed was caused by the robbers.

The *Detroit Free Press*, on Wednesday, March 7, 1894, noted, "Every person in Dexter was greatly surprised over Gregory's confession. If there was an exemplary young man in the village, it was Gregory, who neither drank, smoked nor had any vices."

The *Washtenaw Evening Times*, on Wednesday, March 7, 1894, reported:

> *Young Gregory will be brought to trial for the crime. He is now very sick at home, Dr. Vaughan being called to attend him this morning. His wife is prostrated and under a physician's care and his grandmother is also prostrated with grief, and her condition excites considerable alarm. Mr. and Mrs. J.V.N. Gregory, the young man's parents, are also sick as the result of the excitement.*

The *Ann Arbor Register* reported on Thursday, March 15, 1894, that Gregory was an "imbecile," as his "mind left him" after the robbery. "Orla C. Gregory's grandmother on his mother's side, Mary Paul, hanged herself

RES. OF THE HON. C.S. GREGORY, *DEXTER, MICH.*

The home of C.S. Gregory, the grandfather of Orla C. Gregory, with whom he had been close. *From* Combination Atlas Map of Washtenaw County, Michigan.

at Auburn, N.Y., while insane," continued the account. "The belief is that Orla Gregory, who was a favorite of his grandfather, Hon. C.S. Gregory, has brooded over the fact that nothing was left to him by his will until his mind become unbalanced."

In the end, the bank chose not to prosecute Gregory, as they believed he had acted on an insane impulse and all of the money was recovered.

6

"THEY SHINED ME"

THE MURDER OF JAMES RICHARDS

James Richards was an eccentric farmer who lived on an eighty-acre farm three miles northeast of Dixboro. He had lived on this farm since he arrived from England in 1852, when he was twenty-five years old. On the farm, Richards worked hard, living only on the necessities of life and choosing to live apart from others. He saved his money and kept it hidden in the small log shanty that was his home. Rumors spread that he was wealthy and had a fortune hidden in his home. Richards most likely never knew how much money he had, as he could neither read nor write and had trouble counting past the number four.

Then on the evening of August 12, 1880, Richards returned home, and as he entered the shanty, a man came up behind him and tried to knock him to the ground. They were engaged in a lively fight for a time, and then two more men who had been hiding came up and joined the fight.

The *Ann Arbor Argus* reported on Wednesday, August 18, 1880:

> One of these struck Richards down with a heavy club, and the two others then blindfolded and gagged him and bound his hands and feet. In the tussle, the key to the door had been lost, and one of the thieves accordingly cut out a windowpane and unlocked the window. They then handed in Richards through the window and, by placing some bedclothes on the floor, made a comfortable place on which they proceeded to place him. They then rifled his pockets and searched the house.

Then the men carried off an unknown amount of money that Richards had hidden in the cellar. The two failed to find the $120 Richards had on his person.

It was quite dark at the time of the robbery, so Richards was unable to give a description of the men and later said he did not think he could identify them.

As a result of the robbery, Richards went insane and was sent to the asylum in Pontiac. John W. Nanry was appointed the guardian of Richards, and while searching the shanty, he found large amounts of money hidden in cans, bottles and the wall. Many of the bills Nanry found were ruined by age, and mice had chewed many. Still, Nanry was able to deposit about $1,000 in the Ann Arbor Savings Bank. Richards remained at the asylum for three years, leaving when he was cured. He then returned to his shanty and resumed his former life. He lived a life of peace and quiet until January 1897.

"The farm was stocked with a good team of horses, a cow, a calf and nineteen sheep. He worked the farm but little, using it mainly for grazing

SCENE OF THE RICHARDS MURDER.

JAMES RICHARDS AND THE HOUSE IN WHICH HE WAS MURDERED.

James Richards and the shack he was murdered in. *From the* Washtenaw Evening Times, *October 21, 1897.*

purposes for the stock he kept upon it. The neighbors speak kindly of him. He never bought anything without paying for it on the spot. He bought what he wanted, but he wanted little," reported the *Ann Arbor Argus* on Friday, February 5, 1897.

The shanty where Richards lived was made of hewn logs; it was two stories tall but in fact comprised one story and a huge attic. Richards used only the lower floor, which was divided into two rooms and a pantry. The *Ann Arbor Argus* noted:

> *The huge beams across the room are just six feet, three inches from the flooring. It was almost barren of furniture. The bed took up one half of the little bedroom in the east side of the house. In the living room was a cook stove, a small table, a barrel of cider and an Ann Arbor Brewing Co.'s keg of beer, two or three chairs, and the pantry contained a number of jugs. Under the flooring was a meal bin. There were very few old dishes, a couple of spoons, a knife and fork, a shaving mug and razor, plenty of firewood on each side of the stove, a pitchfork, an axe and a shovel. The flooring was absolutely destitute of covering but had evidently been occasionally cleaned. In the attic, there were a number of rags, corn, etc.*

The shanty was located a quarter of a mile and two fields from the road; yet the shanty, which was on an elevation, was visible from the road, and a nearby house could be seen from the shanty.

The Second Attack

On the evening of January 30, 1897, Richards put out the light around 9:00 p.m. and lay down on his bed, fully dressed. Then there was a knock on the door. Richards asked who was there. Someone said they wanted to see Richards and get warm. Richards said he would not let them in unless they told him who they were.

At this, the men outside flashed a light from a lantern through the window to find Richards. Richards jumped around the room to keep out of the light, and as he did this, he took hold of a pitchfork.

Unable to find Richards with the light, the men went get sticks to break the door down. Richards watched as the men went to his wood pile and searched for what they needed. One of the men grabbed a stick that was

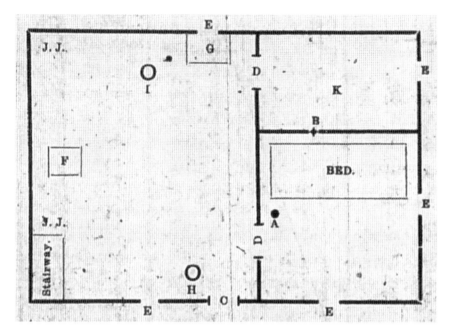

A diagram of the house where Richards was murdered. "In the diagram, the letter A represents where Richards stood when shot. B represents where the bullet, which passed through him, struck the board partition. C is the only outer door of the house and D the bedroom door, through which the bullet was fired. The various small windows, marked E, were partially boarded up and many of the panes filled with old rags. F is where the old cook stove was located, beside which Richards passed the night, and G the small table. H is a cider barrel and I a beer keg." *From the* Ann Arbor Argus, *February 5, 1897.*

over a foot in circumference to use as a battering ram. Another man picked up a stick to ward off the pitchfork. Then they went to break down the door. It may have been at this time that the first gunshot was fired. This shot came from a .32-caliber revolver and embedded itself in the door, the boards of which were made of elm.

Richards used the pitchfork to fight the men off. The men used the door to shield themselves from the pitchfork. As the men used the door as a shield, they kept the light from the lantern centered on Richards's eyes to blind him.

"We want only your money," shouted one of the men. "Let up with the pitchfork and we won't hurt you." Richards continued to put up a brave fight until the second shot was fired. This shot was fired from an ugly .44-caliber revolver. The shot was fired from just outside the door or from just inside the shanty. Richards was struck by the bullet as he stood inside his bedroom.

The *Ann Arbor Argus* reported:

The bullet went entirely through his body, entering just below the breast and passing out near the hip and entering a heavy board back of the bed. To gain some idea of the terrific force of the bullet, it may be well to state that Richards was very warmly dressed. He had on two jackets a vest and very heavy undershirt. One of the jackets and the vest were [made] of a sort of canvas lined with heavy, coarse flannel. Through all this clothing, the bullet plowed its way twice, besides passing through the body and six feet beyond, yet having force enough to embed itself in a hard board.

The shot caused the fight to end, and the two men took Richards's money. They did not search the shanty but seemed to know where to look.

Once the men were gone, Richards lit a lamp, filled the stove with firewood and lay down on the floor by the stove. Here, alone, he passed the night, his blood seeping out of his body.

Richards lay alone on the floor, bleeding, and not until the next day, Sunday, did anyone stop by. Around 1:00 p.m., Henry Tolbert stopped by to see Richards. Tolbert had been hunting rabbits and stopped by the shanty and knocked on the door. Richards called Tolbert into the shanty. When Tolbert asked Richards what was wrong, Richards said he was sick. Then Richards asked Tolbert to "please let the chickens out and feed them."

After Tolbert had done this and returned to the shanty, he asked Richards, "How long have you been sick, Jimmie?"

Then Richards told Tolbert he had been robbed and shot. Then Richards asked Tolbert to go to John Shankland's place to get him a loaf of bread.

Soon, others came to help, and Dr. Jane A. Walker arrived from Salem and had Richards removed to the house of a neighbor, where she could better care for him.

Richards said one of the two men who robbed him was taller than the other and that both wore long coats. He said he did not think he could recognize the men if he saw them. When Richards was asked how much money was stolen, he said only, "They got enough."

Richards died at 7:30 a.m. on Monday, February 1, 1897.

James Talbert

James Talbert, or Henry Tolbert, the African American neighbor who found the dying Richards. *From the* Washtenaw Evening Times, *October 22, 1897.*

Investigation

Harris Ball was the Washtenaw County coroner who oversaw the inquest into the Richards murder. *From the* Washtenaw Evening Times, *October 22, 1897.*

The investigation determined that on Saturday night, three men had driven up to the property in a cutter with a sidebar and a single sharp-shod horse, possibly a fast one, and opened the gate by the road. Then they drove the cutter to the second gate and hitched the horse to the gate. One of the three men stayed with the horse and cutter, while the other two made their way across the field by a circuitous route to avoid a marsh. They clearly knew the lay of the land. The two hid behind a small hill and rack, where they were able to watch the shanty. There, they watched and waited for Richards to put out his light.

The inquest was held on Thursday, February 4, 1897. The jury returned a verdict of: "James Richards came to his death at the house of Frank Dures in the township of Superior on the first day of February 1897 about 7:30 a.m. from the effect of a pistol shot received sometime during the night of January 30, 1897, at his home on his farm in the township of Superior; said shot being fired by someone unknown to the jury and for the purpose of robbery."

Marshal Peterson arrested three men in Plymouth for the murder of James Richards on Saturday, February 13, 1897. The three men were William Larkins, Rupert Jones and Edward Lyons. Peterson was assisted in the arrest by Deputy Sheriffs Eldert and Sweet, who had been shadowing the three for at least three days before the arrest.

On the night of the murder, the three men had hired a rig from the Tennay's livery stable in Plymouth and were absent from there from 9:30 p.m. to 2:00 a.m., plenty of time to drive the ten miles to Richards's farm and back.

The three men said they had been drinking when they set out for Northville, Novi and Farmington that night. They said when they reached Northville, the hotel was closed and the lights were out. Then the three went on to Novi, where they knew the bartender. There, the hotel was closed, and no one responded to their calls. From Novi, they went to

Farmington but were unable to get into a hotel there. Finally, they returned to Plymouth.

On Monday, February 15, 1897, Marshal Peterson and ex-sheriff Brenner traveled the route the three said they had taken. The clerk at the hotel in Northville said he was awake until 1:00 a.m. The proprietor and clerk at Novi said the lights were on until 11:30 p.m. and that no one had tried to get in. The proprietor of the hotel at Farmington said the three, who he knew, did not try to get in his place that night. The tollgate operator on the road to Farmington said no such rig passed through the gate that night.

EX-MARSHAL PETERSON.

Ex-marshal Patterson, who aided the investigation of the Richards murder. *From the Washtenaw Evening Times, October 21, 1897.*

"Larkins owns up to wearing rubber boots, Lyons to wearing pointed shoes with pointed rubbers and Jones pointed shoes without rubbers. At the Richards house were found tracks of a man with rubber boots and of another with pointed shoes and rubbers, and where the horse was tied were tracks of a third man with pointed shoes and no rubbers," reported the *Ann Arbor Argus* on Friday, February 19, 1897.

A .44-caliber revolver was found on Larkins when he was arrested. This was the same caliber as the shot that killed Richards. Larkins's wife said he had fired the weapon twice the day before the murder. Officers suspected he was testing the gun to be sure it worked. When Larkins was arrested, one chamber of the revolver was empty. His wife also said he owned a lantern but that it was now missing.

Larkins and his wife had been married the previous Thanksgiving. His wife had lived on a farm near the one owned by Richards, and Larkins came to know Richards well, it was said, and had driven stock out of his farm.

Because the stories of the three conflicted, Peterson requested that they be kept apart so that they could not to get together and agree on a story. When Peterson called at the jail a few days later, he found the three together. For this reason, a few days later, Jones was moved to the jail in Ypsilanti.

The three were arraigned for the murder of Richards on the morning of Thursday, February 18, 1897, before Justice Gibson. Over one hundred citizens of Plymouth, as well as all the farmers who had lived near Richards, arrived to watch the proceedings. The arraignment had to be moved to the circuit court room, and that was soon filled to overflowing.

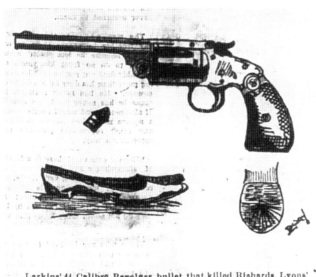

Larkins' 44 Calibre Revolver, bullet that killed Richards, Lyons' rubbers, heel of footprint.

Larkins's .44-caliber revolver, the bullet that killed Richards, Larkins's rubbers and the heel of a footprint were entered into evidence at the trial. *From the* Washtenaw Evening Times, *October 26, 1897.*

Defense attorney Starkweather of Northville asked for an immediate hearing and said to a man that the people of Plymouth believed that the three were innocent. John P. Kirk, the prosecutor, told the court that the case was not ready for trial. "After considerable sparring," reported the *Washtenaw Evening Times*, "the date for formal examination was set for March 9 at 9 a.m. The prisoners were then remanded to jail and, after several minutes spent in receiving the hearty greetings of their many friends, were locked up again."

The preliminary examination of the three was resumed on Tuesday, March 9, 1897. Marshal Peterson testified that the three had told him about the night of the murder but that the stories did not align. Larkins, said Peterson, told him they went to Northville for a lark. Lyons said they went to pick up a music stand. Jones claimed they went to have a time. Peterson also told the court of the tracks found at the Richards farm and of the careful measurements he made of these tracks.

Another witness called was Frank Kingsbury, a farmer who lived west of Plymouth who said that on the night of the murder, he was passed by a one-horse cutter with three men in it. "His statement could not be shaken in any particular. He was unable, at that time, to recognize the occupants of the cutter," reported the *Washtenaw Evening Times* on Wednesday, March 10, 1897.

In the end, the three were bound over for trial in the circuit court, with the trial set for the October term.

How the three came under suspicion was never explained, but several newspapers reported that it was due to a startlingly realistic dream a woman in Plymouth had on the night of the murder. On the night of the murder, the woman dreamed she saw William Larkins, Ed Lyons and Rupert Jones get in a cutter and drive to a place in the country, which corresponded to Richards's shanty. The three men got out of the cutter, and two went into the shanty, but what happened in the shanty, she could not say. Then she said the two hurried out of the shanty and got into the cutter, and the three returned to Plymouth. "The next morning, the lady told Mrs. Jones about her dream," reported the *Ann Arbor Argus* on Friday, March 5, 1897. "She was asked not to say anything, as Mrs. Jones's son was out that night, and the dream might cause suspicion, but the dream was so real to the lady that she could not help telling other friends—not, however, because she suspected there was any truth to it but because it was so realistic."

In truth, the dream had nothing to do with arrest of the three; Sheriff Peterson did not learn of the dream until after the three were already under arrest.

Another subject of interest to the community concerning the case was the question of how securely the prisoners were kept in the jail. Three young men said they had seen Rupert Jones in Fred Brown's saloon around nine o'clock on a Saturday morning, asking for some bottled beer while unattended by an officer. The back door of Fred Brown's saloon ran along an alley that also ran along the jail.

Marshal Peterson swore in an affidavit that he had seen Larkins on

Sherif Judson

William Judson was the sheriff of Washtenaw County from 1895 to 1898. *From the* Washtenaw Evening Times, *October 21, 1897.*

March 15 in the jail yard without an officer in attendance. Further, Peterson claimed he had seen Rupert Jones alone in the hall of the jail with the door unlocked. This meant that the prisoner could come and go as he wished. Peterson added that "in spite of Mr. Judson's belief in the innocence of the prisoners, he is making no effort at finding the guilty parties."

Sheriff Judson obtained a statement from the bartender of the saloon, stating that Jones had not been in the saloon at any time on Saturday. Judson also secured a statement from his deputy that the three had never been out of the personal supervision of the officers since they were placed in custody.

While scoffing at the story and affidavits of Marshal Peterson, the sheriff said that Jones had been out of his cell several times but always in the company of a deputy or himself. A few days before, he had been taken to a Huron Street barbershop to have his hair cut and was taken for a little walk on another occasion, but the story of Jones hanging around saloons unaccompanied is "emphatically denied," reported the *Ann Arbor Argus* on March 19, 1897.

Around the same time, Washtenaw County probate court judge Newkirk received a letter from an attorney in Axminster, England, concerning the estate of James Richards. The attorney, Mr. W. Forward, stated that the daughter of Richards and Temperance Board, Mrs. Sarah Pierce, was illegitimate, as Richards and Board had never been married. Under Michigan law at that time, an illegitimate child could inherit property from their mother but not their father, unless their father had filed with the probate judge a properly witnessed document to acknowledge the relationship. Richards had never done this. There were, however, letters from Richards to Pierce that had been written by someone else, as Richards could not write, acknowledging the relationship. "If the estate goes to court and is decided against the daughter, the property will go to a wealthy sister who lives in the northern England. The letter states that the daughter is in destitute circumstances and has a young family to support," reported the *Ann Arbor Register* on Thursday, March 18, 1897.

In the end, Judge Newkirk decided that the estate of James Richards should go to Pierce. This decision was based on the letters that had been found in Richards's shanty. The *Ann Arbor Register* reported on Thursday, March 24, 1898:

> *A letter from the girl's mother was pathetic in the extreme. She and Richards expected to be married, and, when a child was born to them, she went to live at the home of his parents for a year till trouble with his father caused James to leave for America. After reaching here, he often wrote her to come, but she feared the voyage, which was opposed by her parents.*
>
> *Judge Newkirk decided that since the parties had intended marriage; and had lived together, and since the father had acknowledged his daughter, the relation was a "common law marriage," and the child legitimate.*

THE CASE COMES TO COURT

Prosecuting attorney Andrew J. Sawyer Jr. opened the case against the three accused. *From the* Washtenaw Evening Times, *October 21, 1897.*

The trial of the three opened on the morning of Tuesday, October 19, 1897, with prosecutor Sawyer describing in great detail the last hours of James Richards life, including how he cared for his stock and went to bed with his clothes on. Sawyer told the court of the fight between Richards and the two robbers and their flight after the taking of the money. He talked at length about the tracks found by the shanty and of the alibi of the three.

Henry Talbert was the first witness called to the stand, and he told of finding Richards the next day, feeding his chickens and going for help. The next witness was Dr. Jane Walker, whom the *Washtenaw Evening Times,* on Wednesday, October 20, 1897, described as "a genteel-looking middle-aged lady." "She told where the ball had entered Mr. Richards's body, puzzling Mr. Sawyer and the jury by the use of some pretty big words. She had had the bullet in her possession, with which the wound had evidently been made….She judged the wound necessarily fatal, although she had not so stated at the time," noted the account.

John Shankland was questioned and said Richards attempted to describe the men who robbed him and said, "'Both were youngish and wore long overcoats with the collars turned up. One of them had a light mustache.' Further than this, he did not know."

Under cross-examination, Shankland said he had heard a rumor concerning the robbery that had occurred years before. He said the rumor "connected more persons than the one that is dead." "Mr. Sawyer warned the defense that if they persisted in opening the question of the alleged confession in regard to the previous robbery, he should take advantage of the opening to show that it connected the mother of one of the defendants with this robbery."

The defense objected to Mr. Sawyer making this statement before the jury, and the court reprimanded him for doing so. "The defense were allowed to ask the question, but the prosecution was denied the privilege of going into the matter by the court," reported the *Washtenaw Evening Times* on Thursday, October 21, 1897.

Shankland said he had not told the sheriff and his deputies all he had known at the time and was glad he had not done so. He could not explain why he was glad he had not told all he knew. He said he answered all the questions he was asked.

The defense then produced a letter from the files of the probate court from an official in England. The official claimed that John Briston, formerly of Washtenaw County, said he knew who had murdered Richards. At this, Sawyer jumped to his feet to say that the letter was fraudulent and intended only to clear the defendants. "The discussion as to its admission as competent evidence was heated," noted the *Washtenaw Evening Times* on Friday, October 22, 1897. "Judge Kinne finally got a chance to speak and overruled the evidence."

Shankland admitted under questioning that he had not entered the item of $1,237, which was in the back of his inventory of the Richards property. He said he did not think he was obliged to list the money in his inventory.

After a recess of five minutes, more witnesses were called to testify and were questioned about visiting Richards the day after he had been shot. The witnesses were asked about his statements and about the tracks in the snow. Probate judge Newkirk was called to the stand and said Mr. Shankland had brought him the bank books of Richards with the record of the money he had in the bank. The defense again brought forth the letter from England that stated John Briston knew who had committed the murder. After some quibbling among the lawyers, Judge Newkirk was allowed to say he had received such a letter. A later witness would testify that Briston had left the United States for England in November, two months before the murder.

When court reconvened the next morning, on Thursday, October 21, 1897, Daniel Marr of Superior Township was called to the stand and said he had visited Richards's shanty around 4:00 p.m. on the day after the shooting. Then he said he went to where Richards had been taken. There, he heard Richards say he was attacked by two young men, one a little larger than the other. Richards said the two men had worn long overcoats. Marr heard Richards say something about a light flashing through his window and that he saw the men standing in front of his house. After Marr, more witnesses were called, and each was asked about the tracks in the snow.

A Frank Klugsbury was called to the stand on Friday, October 22, 1897. He said he lived about three miles from Plymouth. "On the night Richards

LARKIN'S BOOTS

JONES.   LARKINS.   LYONS.
THE THREE SUSPECTS.

Left: As footprints were found in the snow at the scene of the crime, Larkins's boots were entered into evidence during the trial. *From the* Washtenaw Evening Times, *October 21, 1897.*

Right: The three defendants on trial, *(from right to left)* William Larkins, Rupert Jones and Edward Lyons. *From the* Washtenaw Evening Times, *October 28, 1897.*

was murdered, he was calling at the house of a friend named Root. Leaving about 11:30, he started toward Plymouth, driving at an ordinary road gait. On the way, three men in a cutter passed him. He could not identify the men," noted the *Washtenaw Evening Times.*

Witnesses were called who were barkeepers at the saloons and hotels where the three said they had stopped on the night of the murder. All said that they did not see them that night.

George Eldert said he saw Larkins in Adams Saloon in December and had a conversation with him. During the course of the conversation, Larkins showed him a large revolver and said, "Well, here is something that'll bring me either money or blood." Under cross-examination Eldert said that he thought the revolver was to be used for "its accustomed purpose—that of killing cattle." Larkins, it was noted, was a butcher.

Hattie Seeley said she operated a tollgate between Novi and Farmington on the night of the murder until 11:30 p.m., and she said no cutter with three men passed through during that time. Her husband, George, took the stand after her but added nothing to the evidence. "On cross-examination, witness admitted driving through gate at least one night since the present keeper took charge and finding the gate open when he reached it," noted the *Washtenaw Evening Times* on October 22, 1897. Those who wished to avoid the tollgate could do so without going more than a mile and a half out of their way.

Colonel Atkinson was the attorney for the accused at the trial. *From the* Washtenaw Evening Times, *October 26, 1897.*

Lizzie Finch was called to the stand, but Sawyer refused to question her, as she had declined to talk with him about the case. Because she had not talked with him before the trial, he had nothing to ask her. Atkinson protested, saying it was the duty of the prosecution to examine the witness. The court declined to interfere, and Lizzie Finch was excused.

John Ridout was called to the stand and said he had become acquainted with the three defendants while in jail. "I was in jail with these prisoners," said Ridout. "One day, Mrs. Larkins came and talked with her husband and said, 'You know you're guilty, and you better say so. I can help you get off easy.'" Ridout said he had heard Jones say to Larkins, "I wouldn't live with such a woman. She would convict anybody." Under cross-examination Ridout said, "I've been in jail so many times, I can't count them or all the crimes I can't think of." In answer to a question concerning his character and honesty, he said: "Yes, I'm a liar—a common liar like the rest of you."

The next witness sworn in was former marshal Peterson, who had been the detective who investigated the case and arrested the three accused. Peterson told the court of the investigation and of finding tracks in the snow the day after the murder. He said the tracks at the shanty were fairly well preserved. "Saw mark in the heel of the rubber track at house. Told others that it was of importance and made drawing of the same on back of bank check. Made design from right foot. Rubbers were produced and identified as those given the witness [Peterson] by the sheriff and said to belong to Lyons."

Peterson said he made the measurements and recorded them on a copy of the *Ypsilanti Sentinel*. The marks on the newspaper, Peterson said, had not been changed. A large revolver had been found at the Larkins house, and Larkins had acknowledged the revolver as his own. Peterson said he examined the tracks at the second gate. These tracks, said Peterson, looked like the tracks found near the shanty. The wear shown by the tracks was similar to the wear on Larkins's boots. Peterson also told of the arrest of the three and recounted their stories of that night.

Under cross-examination, Peterson said he first saw Lizzie Finch when he went to the Larkins house. She and Mrs. Larkins refused to speak to him. The *Washtenaw Evening Times* reported on Monday, October 25, 1897:

> *No one assisted to take measure of tracks. Did not tell sheriff. Was lack of sympathy between sheriff and witness. Judson was enemy of his ever since he was made sheriff. Did not feel unkindly toward Ball. Had been opposed by sheriff's force while he was marshal. This part of the examination was not concluded until the hostility existing between city and county offices at that time was fully exploited.*

Washtenaw County sheriff William Judson was called to the stand and said he had made measurements of the tracks by cutting notches on a stick. He said he had never tried to compare the measurements to the feet of the defendants. Sheriff Judson said he had always tried to help Peterson and always kept Peterson informed as to what his deputies were doing. He said it was not true that the prisoners had played cards in the corridor of the jail.

After Sheriff Judson was excused, the defense requested that the prosecution be compelled to call Lizzie Finch to the stand. The court denied the request.

The prosecution rested, and the defense opened by calling Lizzie Finch to the stand. She said she knew Peterson, who had called on her at the Larkins house in Plymouth. Finch said she had been at the Larkins house for four weeks before the murder of Richards. Larkins, she said, left the house on the night of the murder around 8:45 p.m. and returned home just before 3:00 a.m. Jones came home with him and was drunk. She helped Larkins take his shoes off and put him on the lounge, where he slept. Mrs. Larkins had the revolver when Larkins was away, and she told Finch they need not be afraid, as she had the gun.

Under cross-examination, Finch said she did not remember keeping house at Ypsilanti with Mrs. Larkins. The Larkins house was comfortably furnished, Finch said. She admitted knowing a John Birch but denied being in his house when his wife was away. Mrs. Birch, Finch said, did not find her at the house and did not make her leave with nothing to wear but a bed quilt.

Finch said she had known Jones for three years. Jones, she said, came to see her. She and Jones were engaged to be married. Jones sometimes stayed all night.

After Finch, the defense called a number of witnesses who testified to the good character of the three defendants. Additional witnesses were called who had been at the Richards shanty after the shooting and said they had not seen anyone take measurements of the tracks in the snow. The defense called several witnesses who said they had often found the tollgate between Farmington and Novi open at night. A few witnesses said they had seen a cutter, like the one the three defendants had rented that night, on the road.

The defense rested on Wednesday, October 27, 1897.

The attorneys made their closing arguments, and this was followed by Judge Kinne addressing the jury. "The evidence against the defendants in this case," explained Judge Kinne, "is what is known as circumstantial evidence, and it now rests with you to determine from a careful consideration of the same whether or not in your minds it had produced a conviction of their guilt or of their innocence." Judge Kinne concluded by saying, "You will discharge all passion or prejudice from your minds and act in this matter impartially, fearlessly, and conscientiously, influenced by no other consideration than a determination to reach such a verdict as shall be justified by the evidence and the law."

The next morning, ten o'clock, the jury returned a verdict of "not guilty." The *Washtenaw Evening Times*, on Friday, October 29, 1897, concluded:

> *As soon as the announcement was made, the crowd in the court room broke into a perfect storm of cheers, surrounding the three prisoners and tendering their heartiest and loudest congratulations. Judge Kinne and Sheriff Judson rapped repeatedly for quiet, and when quiet was partially restored, the judge sharply reprimanded the crowd. Then followed the formal polling of the jury and the discharge of the prisoners. Thus ended one of the most hotly contested criminal trials Washtenaw County has ever seen.*

LIFE AFTER TRIAL

Larkins, Jones and Lyons returned to Plymouth and their normal lives. Rupert Jones was expected to marry Lizzie Finch but instead deserted her. She, then with child, faced disgrace and ruin. However, she was not alone in the world. Jacob Straub, described as an honest young German, was in love with her. "Others kicked her," he said, "but I pitied her, and we were married." After the birth of her child, Lizzie was gravely ill and was told she was dying. At this, she became greatly agitated, and between gasps for breath, she exclaimed, "O, I must confess, I must, I want to be forgiven!" When a notary was present, Lizzie made the following statement:

> *William Larkins, Ed Lyons and Rupert Jones of Plymouth are the murderers of James Richards. The murder occurred January 30, 1897. I was, at that time, living at the home of William Larkins in Plymouth. Larkins and Jones left Larkins's house about 9:00 p.m., January 30, and returned about 3:00 a.m., January 31, Larkins wearing felts and rubbers and Jones wearing a pair of Larkins's rubber boots.*
>
> *Jones afterward told me that they went to the home of James Richards and tried to scare him by going from window to window with a dark lantern and, finding they could not accomplish anything by that means, they tried to break in the door with a rail, or post, or something of that kind. Finding that Richards fought them back, they shot through the door with a .32-caliber revolver.*
>
> *Then Richards seemed to cease fighting, but when they broke down the door and entered, they found Richards in the corner of the room where the fire was. He fought them with a pitchfork, and they used the same instrument with which they broke down the door. During the battle, the old man got Lyons cornered and would have killed or injured him but for Larkins, who shot Richards with a .44-caliber revolver. Then Richards told them the money was in a sack in the bed tick, and while Larkins and Lyons were fighting him, Jones got the sack. They were frightened and hurried away, and Jones says he dropped the sack somewhere between the house and rig. The dark lantern that they used was cut to pieces by Jones and placed under the kitchen. The boots worn by Jones were sold to a rag peddler by Larkins, while those wore by Larkins were burned up.*
>
> *The amount of money taken was seventy dollars, of which Larkins and Lyons each got twenty dollars and Jones thirty dollars, he keeping ten dollars that the others knew nothing about.*

Lizzie Finch did not die but recovered and repeated her statement to a reporter from the *Ann Arbor Register*, which published the statement on Thursday, March 24, 1898.

Lizzie Finch also had something to say about how Sheriff Judson ran the county jail. She said Sheriff Judson was supposed to keep the three men apart and that Jones was kept in a room on the third floor. Jones was not confined to this room; according to Finch, he had a key and could come and go as he pleased. Lizzie Finch said she would visit Jones at the jail when she pleased, and her shame, she said, was a result of these visits. "I have stayed in the room with him," said Lizzie Finch, "from three in the afternoon till nine at night, and no one else was there. My mother went sometimes, and she knows that Jones had a key. Why, one time, he went to a saloon and got two bottles of beer. One he drank and the other he passed in to one of the boys. They had a place where they could pass in stuff to drink. It was in one of the south windows, I think."

Lizzie Finch was not the only one to visit Jones. According to her statement, "one day, H. Weeks, Orson Moore, and some other men from Plymouth came to the jail. They all went to Jones's room and took whiskey, which they drank there."

Lizzie's mother, Mrs. Rose Bryant, was asked if her statement was true. Mrs. Bryant said it was and added more information. "Larkins," she said, "came to our house in January. He was drunk and in some way showed that he had a .32-caliber revolver. My husband said: 'Is that the gun that killed Richards?' 'No,' he answered, 'but here it is.' And pulled out a .44 Smith & Wesson."

When questioned by the reporter from the *Ann Arbor Register*, William Larkins said, "The girl is telling this to get even with Jones. It is not true. I did tell Bryant that I had the gun that killed Richards, but I said it as a joke. It is true that Jones had a key to his room in the jail and went in and out as he pleased and took his girl to the room as often as he wanted to."

Lyon said, "Yes, Jones had a key, and he could have got out if he wanted to. He took Lizzie Finch to his room when he pleased, and I shouldn't wonder if she tells the truth when she says her disgrace began there."

As the three men had been found not guilty at trial, no further action could be taken against them.

At the time that the statement made by Lizzie Finch was published, newspapers were covering the growing tension between the United States and Spain. The battleship the USS *Maine* had been destroyed by an explosion in Havana Harbor. At the outbreak of war, William Larkins,

Rupert Jones and Edward Lyon enlisted in the army. The three were discharged after the war in 1899.

William Larkins worked as a butcher and was arrested in February 1901 for receiving sheep stolen from a farm in Salem Township. In May that year, he was sentenced to two years in Jackson Prison. He moved to North Dakota in 1903 but must have returned soon after, as he was arrested for being drunk and disorderly in November 1904. Then in 1905, he was injured in an accident when he was scalded by boiling water while butchering hogs. Then in 1906, he was convicted of stealing ten chickens and sent to jail for ninety days. Larkins died at the Ypsilanti State Hospital on April 24, 1941. He had been an inmate of the hospital for five years. His death certificate lists insanity as a contributing cause of death.

After the war, Rupert Jones returned to his occupations of music and barbering. He died on September 4, 1914, at the military hospital in Marion, Indiana.

Edward Lyons died on January 31, 1944.

7

DEATH OF AN UNKIND FATHER

Mrs. Weid was a midwife who was sometimes called out all night, as she was on the evening of Saturday, January 2, 1910. After the birth, Mrs. Weid must have felt a sense of satisfaction at a job well done. This sense of satisfaction most likely turned to apprehension on Sunday morning as she approached her home at 144 Phillips Street in Ann Arbor. This was a pleasant and comfortable house, but there was good reason for Mrs. Weid to be concerned as she returned home.

Her husband, Frederick, who was forty-four years of age and said to be a fine-looking man, had worked during the summer as a mason tender for Sauer & Co. By January 1910, he was employed as a laborer at the University of Michigan.

Frederick was also an excessive drinker of hard cider, sometimes drinking as much as a gallon a day. He was also a jealous man who would accuse his wife of being out all night for other purposes. Sure enough, upon her return home, there was a quarrel, and hot words passed between the two.

Frederick had been quarreling with their five children before her arrival, their eighteen-year-old son, August, their eldest, seeming to be a great source of anger to Frederick. As Frederick and August quarreled, the father threatened to kill the son and got out a shotgun for that purpose. Finding the gun unloaded, he set it aside and went in search of shells. After Frederick had left the room, August picked up the gun and removed the hammer. Then August placed the gun back where his father had left it.

Returning to the room, Frederick picked up the gun and found the hammer had been removed, which did not improve his mood. Filled with rage, Frederick took up a butcher knife and chased August to the house of a neighbor.

This was likely the scene that greeted Mrs. Weid when she arrived home.

Once the chase of August and the quarrel with his wife were over, Frederick seemed less quarrelsome but remained sullen and gloomy. Still, he did not threaten to harm the other children.

He ate dinner and soon after the meal left the house and went to the Van Doren Drugstore on Packard Street. There, he asked for some carbolic acid. He said he wanted it to treat a sore. Mr. Van Doren refused to sell undiluted acid to him. Frederick then ordered a solution of equal parts of glycerine and carbolic acid. Mr. Van Doren sold him an eight-ounce bottle, and Frederick signed the prescription blank.

From the store, Frederick went home, and standing on the doorstep, he raised the bottle to his lips and drank some five ounces of the mixture. Some children who were playing next door saw what he had done and sounded the alarm. The children grabbed the bottle from his hands as Frederick entered the house. He staggered into the house and threw himself on to a couch. There on the couch, in less than five minutes, Frederick died. Drs. Belser and Clark were summoned but could not get to the house in time to do anything.

"Although he died in terrible agony, there is nothing about the body to show how the deed was done, not even the faintest sign of burns about the mouth or on the lips," noted the *Ann Arbor Daily Times News* on Monday, January 3, 1910.

Mrs. Weir was grief-stricken and threw herself on the dead body of her husband, begging him to return to her. All day, she did nothing but wring her hands and beg Frederick to speak to her.

The neighbors had long feared for the safety of Mrs. Weir and the children. They told her it was better that he had killed himself and not lived to murder her or the children. "The children don't all think so," was her reply.

As the quarrels had been going on for a long time, the children had taken sides in the trouble, some sympathizing with the mother and the others with the father.

It was said Frederick had carried some $5,000 worth of insurance.

His funeral was held at the residence on the afternoon of Tuesday, January 4, 1910, with his burial taking place in Bethlehem Cemetery.

8
DEATH AT THE DEPOT

Robert McCormick was at the Michigan Center Depot in downtown Detroit on the evening of Thursday, January 7, 1910, when he ran into Charles Harrington and Charles Billings, friends he had made in reform school. McCormick had been born in Ypsilanti but then lived in Detroit with his family. He described his father as kind of lame. At the age of fourteen, McCormick was sent to the reform school in Lansing. On January 7, 1910, at seventeen years of age, he had just been released from the school. He, Harrington and Billings rode the 9:25 p.m. train from Detroit and arrived at Ypsilanti at 10:15 p.m. The three went to the downtown section of the city and stopped in at the waiting room of the Ypsi-Ann, the interurban or street railroad. They asked the man there what time the next car left for Detroit. The man told them the next car would leave at 11:15 p.m. and that there were fifteen minutes left before it would come.

The three left the waiting room and made their way down Congress Street, now Michigan Avenue, and passed the Switzer Brothers Jewelry Store. They made the decision to rob the store. The reason for the trip to Ypsilanti from Detroit was to find a place to rob. They had come to Ypsilanti to steal from places before.

McCormick, Harrington and Billings went around to the back of the store and pried open a window by taking out two panes of glass. McCormick and Harrington entered the store, leaving Billings outside to act as watchman.

Around 11:15 p.m., William H. Morey, the night watchman, was on patrol and entered the alley behind the Switzer Brothers Jewelry Store. Morey became suspicions that something was going on when he saw Billings

Above: The Interurban Railroad's waiting room on Washing Street, where McCormick, Harrington and Billings stopped before going to the Switzer Brothers Jewelry Store. *Used with the permission of the Ypsilanti Historical Society.*

Opposite, top: The 100 block of West Michigan Avenue, where the Switzer Brothers Jewelry Store was located. *Used with the permission of the Ypsilanti Historical Society.*

Opposite, bottom: Ypsilanti chief of police Milo Gage (*center*) in his office at the Savings Bank Building, or present-day city hall, with Patrolman Tom Ryan (*left*) and Walter Pierce (*right*). *Used with the permission of the Ypsilanti Historical Society.*

run away down the alley. His suspicions were further confirmed when he found that the window at the back of the store broken. Morey entered the store, flashing his bullseye lantern in front of him. He saw McCormick and Harrington crouching in the rear of the store and shouted, "Hands up!"

McCormick and Harrington fired their guns at Morey. A bullet whizzed past Morey's head. Morey then drew his gun and returned fire. One of the young men screamed in pain as he was hit. Harrington had been hit in the wrist. The three exchanged shots until Morey's gun was empty. McCormick decided this was no place for him and made a break for the door. Harrington must have had the same idea, as he made a run for it as well. The two rushed past Morey and escaped through the open door.

Morey then informed Ypsilanti chief of police Milo E. Gage of what had happened, as well as Officers Walter H. Pierce and Thomas Ryan. Word of

the event was sent throughout the city, and everyone who was informed was told to be on the lookout for the three.

Morey went in search of the three, and three hours later, he found Billings at the Michigan Central Depot. Billings claimed he had no knowledge of the attempted robbery. Morey arrested him as a suspect and locked him up in the jail.

After escaping from the jewelry store, McCormick and Harrington made their way to a house on Miles Street, where they built a fire to keep warm and hid until about 5:00 a.m. The two left the house and made their way to the Michigan Central Depot. At the depot, the two made their way to the waiting room. They were seen by Henry C. Miner, the night baggage man, and Morgan J. Emmett, the night ticket agent. Miner and Emmett had been told to be on the lookout for the two.

At the depot was seven-year-old Tom O'Brien, a newspaper delivery boy. He was waiting for the arrival of the morning train and the newspapers from Detroit. Miner asked O'Brien to go into the waiting room and look the two over. O'Brien did as he was asked and told Miner he had never seen the two before. Miner turned to Emmett and said, "There are our men, let's get them."

Miner and Emmett secured revolvers and entered the waiting room. Pointing the revolvers at McCormick and Harrington, they told the two to come with them. Miner took hold of McCormick, and Emmett held on to Harrington, and they led them to the doorway to the baggage room. As they entered the doorway, McCormick broke away from Miner and ran off. Miner went in pursuit of McCormick, firing his gun as he ran after him. Emmett pushed Harrington into the baggage room.

The Michigan Central Railroad Depot as it appeared on the day of the murder, January 7, 1910. *Used with the permission of the Ypsilanti Historical Society.*

When Miner returned to the baggage room alone, Emmett asked, "Did you get him?" Miner did not reply but went to the phone and asked the operator to connect him to "Mr. Gage." This was Milo Gage, the Ypsilanti chief of police.

At his home, Chief Gage answered the phone. The operator told him that the party at the depot had left the receiver down and had left the line. Harrington was then seated in a chair. He rose a few inches from his seat, pointed his gun upward and shot Emmett. As Harrington started to run, Emmett held on to him, and Miner joined the struggle as well. The three stumbled onto the platform and Harrington cried out," Help, help, Bob! Help me!"

At this point, a shot must have been fired, hitting Miner, as he broke away from the struggle and staggered across the tracks, grasping an iron railing and sinking to the ground. Harrington broke away from Emmett and ran toward the east. Emmett stumbled into the ticket office.

HENRY C. MINER

Henry C. Miner, who was the night baggage manager at the depot on the night of January 7, 1910. *From the* Detroit Free Press, *January 8, 1910.*

Tom O'Brien had followed the men to the baggage room, and as the fight had begun, he crouched in a corner of the room.

William Morey, the night watchman, was walking down Cross Street when he heard the sounds of the fight. Running toward the depot, Morey turned a corner and stumbled over the body of Miner in a pool of blood. Morey dragged the body of Miner to one side and then rushed into the depot. There, he found Emmett crumpled on a bench but still alive.

Austine Crane and Charles Caine, an ex-policeman, went in search of McCormick and Harrington. Night watchman Morey continued his hunt for the two as well. Officer Walter Pierce went to Cook's livery and secured a rig; he then started east on Michigan Avenue. Several farmers told Pierce they had seen a man making his way down the road. A small boy told Pierce that a man had tried to sell him a revolver for fifty cents. Pierce went as far as Denton before he began making his way back.

Seeing an interurban car approach, he signaled for the motorman to stop. On the car was Harrington, who was nursing his shattered wrist. Harrington was removed from the car and taken back to Ypsilanti. There, his wrist was treated by Drs. Britton and Hull.

A gunfight and escape from the depot as Morgan Emmett is shot. *From the* Detroit Free Press, *January 8, 1910.*

After the gun battle at the depot, Harrington had stopped at the house of L.H. Pattee, near the depot, and claimed he had fallen off a train. Pattee helped Harrington dress his wrist.

Crane and Caine followed the trail of Robert McCormick and found him riding on an interurban car between Willard's Crossing and Denton. Because of his wounds, McCormick was taken to the homeopathic hospital in Ann Arbor.

The three men had stolen about eighty dollars' worth of fountain pens and inexpensive jewelry from the Switzer Brothers Jewelry Store, all of which was recovered when Harrington and McCormick were arrested.

McCormick confessed to the murder of Miner, and at first, the authorities believed it was McCormick who had fired the fatal shot at Miner. McCormick most likely believed he had killed Miner. It was not until the bullet was removed from the body of Miner that it was discovered Harrington had killed him. Even then, the belief would persist that it was McCormick who murdered Miner.

On the afternoon of Tuesday, January 11, 1910, McCormick and Billings went before Judge George Kenny of the Washtenaw County Circuit Court. McCormick and Billings waived their right to a trial. Judge Kenny held a meeting with the two before appearing in court. Billings was charged with burglary. Billings explained to Judge Kenny that he got into trouble because he was trying to get away from his wife. "My father told me Thursday," said Billings, "that Judge Durfree was going to give me five years because I did not support my wife, and he told me I had better skip for the west. So, I

An interurban car like the one McCormick and Harrington used to make their escape. *Used with the permission of the Ypsilanti Historical Society.*

started, and when I got to the depot, I met McCormick and Harrington and went with them. That's how I got mixed up with it."

McCormick was charged with the murder of Henry Miner. "I suppose there is no escape for me," said McCormick to Judge Kenny. "There is nothing for me to do but to plead guilty." Judge Kenny told McCormick not to plead guilty unless he was guilty.

McCormick replied, "I'm guilty all right."

Then McCormick asked, "Now, how will it be about parole?" A murderer, Judge Kenny explained, was not allowed parole.

"Well," said McCormick, "let us have it over with."

When McCormick and Billings appeared in court, Billings was sentenced to five to ten years in prison. Billings responded with only a quick shift of his quid of tobacco from one cheek to the other. Later, Billings said, "Well, I get out in five years, that will be no worse than if I had that time for nonsupport."

When McCormick heard his sentence to life imprisonment, there was no change in his expression.

Harrington had planned to plead guilty to the charge assault with intent to commit murder but changed his mind after a visit from his sister. She had spent some time with him and urged him to stand trial. "I didn't know he was drifting," she explained to the police. "His father and mother are dead, and I was looking after him, but I must have failed somehow."

The arraignment of Harrington was set for a later date.

Emmett was expected to die from his wounds and was sent to a hospital in Detroit for treatment. There, Emmett began to recover and was able to make a statement. In his statement, Emmett placed the blame for the murder of Miner on Harrington. He told of how McCormick had slipped from Miner at the door to the baggage room and how McCormick had run off with Miner in pursuit. Emmett said he pushed Harrington into the baggage room, where Harrington sat in a chair. Emmett continued:

> And in a minute, Miner came in from the outside and this fellow [Harrington] was sitting down on a chair still. I think Miner's gun was empty. I couldn't see what he was doing, but I think he was reloading his gun. He turned around, and he says to this fellow, "Get up and let us see what you got on you." And the fellow got up out of the chair and pulled his gun and fired on Harry, and Harry went down. Just as he fired, I jumped on to this fellow's back as well as I could.
>
> I reached for the poor devil's throat, and I was going to choke him. Harry, as he fell down, pulled his gun and fired, and I think that the ball hit the robber. Miner jumped up, but in the meantime, this fellow was shooting at Harry all the time. He shot two or three times at Harry.
>
> Then he turned his attention to me. He threw his arm up over his left shoulder. And the gun came right in my face, and I ducked. But he fired just the same, and that ball went into my shoulder. Then he threw the gun over his right shoulder and gave me one in the breast, but I hung on to him. Of course, when I got the ball in the shoulder, that put my left arm out of business, and I couldn't hang on any longer.
>
> In the struggle with the one I had at the door there, I found out that his partner had got away and called him Bob, and that is as much as I know about it.

Harrington, who was being held in the county jail at Ann Arbor, then admitted to the murder of Henry Miner. "I am guilty of the murder of Henry Miner," said Harrington. "Let me plead guilty and get away from here." This led to the question asked by officials at the jail: "How can you and McCormick both be guilty of the murder of Miner?" To this, Harrington replied, "My God, men, I am ready to plead guilty. Let me get out of here. I'll be a maniac in another week." Harrington, it was said, was tormented by the thought that his friend McCormick was in prison for the crime Harrington had committed.

Washtenaw County prosecutor Carl Storm issued a statement concerning the case on Saturday, January 22, 1910. He stated that a charge of murder would be lodged against Harrington at once. It was clear from the statement of Emmett and the evidence that it was Harrington who had fired the fatal shot that killed Miner. Storm wrote:

> *This, however, does not affect McCormick's case, as he also is undoubtedly guilty of the same offense, having been in a concerted scheme with Harrington to escape and kill if necessary to do so. Evidently, these boys gave each other the sign, since they both attempted to escape and fired shots in order to get away. Killing by one of two persons or more, when the result of common plot, would in law, be murder. Therefore, McCormick's case was properly disposed of. Moreover, McCormick admitted the offense and pleaded guilty to it.*

After McCormick and Harrington were arrested, each had made statements in which they confessed to the robbery of the jewelry store and the shooting at the depot. Storm wrote:

> *At that time, because of the conflicts in the statements of the two, it appeared that McCormick had shot Miner and Harrington had shot Emmett. Harrington brazenly calmed this in the presence of McCormick, and McCormick did not deny it. As it now appears, the latter seemed inclined to take his share, if not more, of the blame, and to protect Harrington, while Harrington, on the other hand, tried to shield himself and, in order to do so, tried to make everyone believe McCormick had shot Miner in the baggage room after Miner had made his escape.*

Storm noted:

> *Before we saw Emmett yesterday, Harrington seems to have proven himself most untruthful and unreliable. He not only did not try to shield his "pal" but tried to make him appear much worse than he was.*
>
> *He need not howl so about being in jail a few days or weeks. He probably will spend much of his future time in prison somewhere, so it is immaterial where he is. We could not think of disposing of his case hurriedly unless the most serious charge, murder, was made against him and he pleaded to it, for the public welfare is deeply interested in having these men punished as severely as the law will allow. Desperadoes must not be dealt with lightly so as to encourage others with similar tendencies.*

Storm stated that Harrington had been willing to plead guilty to the charge of assault with intent to commit murder until his sister spoke with him. She, noted Storm, felt sorry for her brother and was deeply interested in his case. Storm, as well as other officials, desired to show her every courtesy. "To have overridden her wishes would have seemed to 'railroad' the man. There has never been a time I know of when he and his council and sister all agreed and consented that he should be guilty to any charge, and I could not well act on his request alone at this time."

The preliminary hearing for Charles Harrington was held in Ypsilanti on February 7, 1910, at the municipal court, Justice Gunn presiding. He arrived on the 1:45 p.m. eastbound interurban car. He was accompanied by his attorney A.J. Sawyer Jr. and was handcuffed to a deputy sheriff. "The lad shows the effect of confinement in the county bastille," noted the *Ypsilanti Daily Press*. "His cheeks are sunken, and an unnatural light is seen in his large brown eyes. His shattered wrist has been causing him considerable trouble, is healing and it is supposed that the pain has had its effect on him physically."

At the hearing, Morgan J. Emmett, who had almost completely recovered from his wound, said, "Charles Harrington is the murderer of Henry Miner."

Harrington was remanded to the county jail without bail to await trial before the circuit court. As Harrington stepped onto the interurban car for the return trip to Ann Arbor, he turned and waved his hand at those standing on the walk.

Robert McCormick had been in the hospital at Jackson Prison since his arrival there. At 2:00 a.m. on March 7, 1910, the day before the trial of Harrington was meant to begin, he made his escape. The guard said he heard McCormick breathing, as if asleep. The guard walked away, but when he returned a few moments later, he found that McCormick, with a second prisoner, had sawed out a bar in a window, made a rope from bedding and climbed down the wall from the fourth-floor window. The two were seen walking east along the railroad tracks. They were found the next day, huddling in a boxcar eight miles from Jackson, and returned to the prison.

The trial of Harrington was quickly over, as his attorney made a motion to change his plea from "not guilty" to "guilty." Harrington was then sentenced to life imprisonment at Jackson.

Harrington did not spend the rest of his life in prison. In 1920, Michigan governor Albert E. Sleeper pardoned him. Harrington was released from prison and then disappeared from the record.

Robert McCormick did spend the rest of his life in prison, as he died of tuberculosis on September 5, 1912. His mother was still living in Detroit at the time, and as soon as she received word of his death, she set out for the prison at Jackson. Inmates of the prison asked permission to give one hundred dollars to his mother so that McCormick might receive a Christian burial. Permission was granted, and the money was turned over to McCormick's mother. The funeral service was held in the Starkweather Chapel at Highland Cemetery on the afternoon of Saturday, September 7, 1912. McCormick's grave is located on the north end of the cemetery. Buried nearby is Henry Miner, the man he was convicted of killing.

9

WHITTAKER JEWELRY STORE ROBBERY

O rval F. Hawkes had a jewelry store in the village of Whittaker, about seven miles south of Ypsilanti, for over thirty years. Hawkes enjoyed a reputation of being a skillful workman, and watches and clocks from all over were taken to him for repair.

His shop was described as a poor, old, rickety place with the Wabash Railroad passing through the village of Whittaker near his shop. The shop was the second place standing across the tracks on the east side of the street. A lumberyard and sawmill were located next to his shop, with a general store across the way, but there was nothing else close to the shop. The shop, it was said, stood in a desolate site.

Hawkes was seventy-three years of age in 1921 and was not married. He lived alone in the back of his shop. In the shop stood two large safes and a lot of his stock on display in showcases.

Around 11:00 a.m. on Sunday, October 30, 1921, a large touring car was parked in front of the shop. Two young men entered the shop and asked to see some watches. Hawkes opened a safe to take some watches out for the men to see. As Hawkes did this, one of the men hit him over the head, knocking him unconscious. The men then tied his feet, bound his hands behind his back and gagged him. He was then carried into the back room, where the men tossed him onto the bed and covered him with blankets. The two men then proceeded to loot the store, filling their pockets with cash, jewelry and Liberty bonds. The value of the loot was about $2,000. The men left the store, got in their car, a Hudson Super Six with red running gear, and drove away.

About an hour after the robbery, Hawkes regained consciousness, and although he was tied to the bed, he managed to wriggle free and untie his legs. He made his way to the door, which he found was locked. Hawkes, with his hands still bound behind him, succeeded in opening a window. Passing through the window, he fell to the ground and began to crawl to a nearby house. As he made his way toward the house, some friends found him and set him free.

At once, a doctor was summoned, and police were informed of the crime. Ypsilanti chief of police John Connors spread the news as soon as he was informed, and the Michigan State Police, Washtenaw County Sheriff's Department and other police agencies were on the lookout for the car. Connors then went to Whittaker to investigate the case. In Whittaker, Hawkes told Connors he would recognize the men who robbed him if he saw them again. Chief Connors visited gas stations and other places and was able to track the car, which was headed toward Detroit, for several miles.

On Monday, October 31, 1921, Connors used the information he had to locate the car in Ecorse. The car belonged to a woman named Veda Sikie, who had the reputation of being a bootlegger. On Sunday, Connors, accompanied by Washtenaw County deputy sheriff Dick Elliott, found that the car that was used by a man named Sam Stanich, who lived at 33 Edith Street in Ecorse. At the house, Connors and Elliott found the car parked in the backyard. Connors and Elliott went to the house and knocked on the door.

"Anybody here?" asked Connors.

"Only my own family," responded Stanich.

"You are a liar," said Connors, "for we just saw two men enter."

"Oh, yes; they are friends of the family," said Stanich.

"Well," said Connors, "you are under arrest." Connors placed handcuffs on Stanich.

As Stanich was talking to Connors, he was wearing a watch and a watch chain. Connors and Elliott noticed that Stanich was trying to do something with his watch chain. They found one of the watches that was stolen from the shop in Whittaker on that watch chain.

At Stanich's house was a Charles Lynbenvoich, who ran a jewelry store at 105 West End Avenue in Detroit. When Lynbenvoich's shop was searched, more of the stolen items were found. As they searched the house, Connors noticed that one of the panel steps on the stairway was loose. The step dropped forward when it was taken up, and behind the step, they found a revolver and a blackjack.

When Stanich was asked what his occupation was, he answered with pride, "Bootlegger." He was listed as such at the county jail.

The next morning in Whittaker, Hawkes positively identified Stanich as one of the men who had robbed him. The trial of Sam Stanich started in December 1921 with the jury selection. The selection of the jury took longer than normal; the panel was exhausted, and attorneys agreed to draw members of the jury from the spectators in the courtroom. Several of the spectators were examined and excused. Then officers were sent out to the street to find men to fill out the jury. When the jury was selected, Stanich's attorney made a motion to have the case dismissed, claiming the arrest of Stanich was done illegally. He noted that the return date on the warrant was November 4, while the date on the complaint was November 5. The motion was denied by the court.

Orval Hawkes took the stand and positively identified Stanich as one of the two men who had robbed him. "I know that is the man," said Hawkes. The defense tried, under cross-examination, to shake Hawkes's belief that Stanich was the man. Hawkes was firm in his belief Stanich was the man who had robbed him. Jewelry found in the Stanich home was identified by Hawkes as his stolen property.

Thomas Hitchingham, a resident of Whittaker, told the court that he saw Stanich leave the store and get into a car with red wheels on the day of the robbery.

John Connors testified that on the day after Stanich was arrested, he was taken to Whittaker. On the way, Stanich asked where they were going. According to Connors, when he was told that he was being taken to where he had been on Sunday, Stanich said, "I didn't hit the old man."

The defense tried to show that Stanich was at home on the Sunday that the LeBlanc brothers returned the car and that Herschel LeBlanc borrowed sixty-eight dollars and offered the stolen jewelry as security.

Sara Stanich, the wife of Sam, took the stand on behalf of her husband. As Mrs. Stanich testified, she fainted.

The case went to the jury, and after being out for nearly twenty hours, they were unable to agree on a verdict. The jury had taken eight votes, of which, seven had a six-to-six ruling for conviction, and the eighth had a seven-to-five ruling.

The case was bound over to the March term of the court.

The jury selection for the second trail of Sam Stanich began on the morning of Tuesday, March 7, 1922. The trail was off to a slow start, as there were so many peremptory challenges set by the defense of the jurors on the first panel that a second panel had to be called. A total of twenty-eight men were excused before a jury of twelve men could be formed. There was good reason to excuse one of those men on the first panel, as he had been dead for a year and a half. One of the men excused from the second panel had been dead for some time as well.

Orval Hawkes recounted the events of the morning he was robbed but stumbled a bit when recalling the events in chronological order. He did, however, identify Stanich as the man who had robbed him. Pointing a finger at Stanich, Hawkes said, "That is the man."

Charles Lynbenvoich, who had been arrested with Stanich and was then testifying for the prosecution, said Stanich had shown him a watch the day of the robbery.

From the witness stand, Stanich claimed he had never been to Whittaker until he was taken there the day after his arrest. He denied that he stated his occupation was bootlegging when asked and said he did not claim that he had not hit the old man when he was told he was being taken to Whittaker. Stanich claimed that he had just moved into the house where he was arrested, so the revolver and blackjack found hidden in the step must have been left by a previous tenant. He further claimed he was the innocent holder of the stolen jewelry, which had been left with him to sell.

Sara Stanich, the wife of Sam, was called to the stand by the defense. The prosecution chose not to cross-examine her. As she was leaving the witness stand, she fainted and fell to the floor while holding a baby in her arms. The child was not harmed. Mrs. Stanich was carried to the jury room, where she recovered.

Judge George Simple, in summing up the case, told the jury about the value of circumstantial evidence, and the prisoner was entitled to acquittal if the prosecution failed to prove its case.

After seventy-two hours of deliberation, the jury asked to be admitted to the court. When entering the courtroom, the members of the jury looked worn and haggard. The jury reported that they were unable to agree on a verdict. Judge Sample ordered the jury back to continue their deliberation until they reached a verdict. The jury returned to their task with heavy hearts. Later that afternoon, the jury returned with a verdict of guilty. Judge Sample sentenced Stanich to twelve to twenty-four years in the prison at Jackson. As the sentence was pronounced, Mrs. Stanich, who had been quietly crying, broke into sobs and was taken from the room by a friend.

10

A LONELY GRAVE FOR HARRY CYB

The Lincoln Consolidated School in Augusta Township stands on the northwest corner of Whittaker and Willis Roads. On the southeast corner, on Friday, September 18, 1925, stood the store and gasoline station owned by Harry Cyb, who was then thirty-five years of age. The building was also home to Cyb, his wife, Mary, and their five children. Cyb, who was Austrian, had owned the store only a short time. In the short time Cyb had owned the store, he had been robbed once or twice, and he had told police he suspected two men named Crossie were the perpetrators.

Around 10:00 p.m. on Friday, September 18, 1925, Harry went in his house by the side door to lie on the bed. Nearby sat his wife, Mary, who was sewing a dress for their little girl. She looked out the kitchen door and saw two cars in the yard. She could see two men in the first car and one man in the second. One of the men in the car asked for Harry. He said he wanted gasoline. Mary told Harry that someone wanted gasoline. Harry got up from the bed and walked through the store to wait on the man. Once the tank was filled with gasoline, the man asked for oil.

Looking through the window in the door leading from the house to the store, Mary saw Harry prepare an ice cream soda for a man she knew only as the "Lord boy." This was Robert Lord, a student at the Michigan State Normal College, now Eastern Michigan University. Lord was employed at a gas station at 15 East Cross Street in Ypsilanti and lived four miles south of Ypsilanti on Whittaker Road.

Harry Cyb's gas station stood on the southeast corner of Whittaker and Willis Roads. The newly built Lincoln Consolidated School building stood on the northeast corner. Pictured is the first school building, which was destroyed by fire less than a year after it opened. The current building stands on the same site. *Used with the permission of the Ypsilanti Historical Society.*

Lord later said he arrived at the store around 10:35 p.m. and talked with Harry for about five minutes. Then Harry went out long enough to put oil in the other men's car. Harry then went into the store with an empty oil bottle to fill it. Harry talked with Lord for four or five minutes and then went outside. "The first noise I heard," later said Lord, "was that of the starting of the car. I noticed it because the driver stepped on it three or four times before the car started and because it made a distinctive noise." Lord continued, "I was leaning against the counter at the back of the room. I could see the windshield, part of the hood and the front seat from where I stood. There were two men in the front seat. I couldn't see anybody else, nor anything on the running board."

Two or three minutes after the car drove away, Lord went outside. He saw an empty oil bottle to the left of where the car had been and a small spot of blood near the bottle. To the right of where the car had been was a larger spot of blood.

Lord tapped on the window of the house to tell Mary that something was wrong—Harry was missing. Lord, Mary and the five Cyb children rushed to the nearby home of Washtenaw County deputy sheriff I.M. Yoder. Because

Yoder did not have a telephone, he, Mary, Lord and the five Cyb children crowded into his car and drove east to the village of Willis. In Willis, Yoder had E.J. Dexter notify the police in Ypsilanti, Detroit and the Michigan State Police in Wayne of Harry's disappearance. Yoder then tried to follow the car, thinking the men were driving to Detroit.

In Ypsilanti, the call was received by Officer Ernest Klavitter, who at once summoned Washtenaw County undersheriff Dick Elliott, as the case was outside the limits of the city. Elliott received the call at 11:20 p.m., and at once left for the store near Lincoln Consolidated School with Klavitter and Officer Herman Oltersdorf. When they arrived at the store, they saw the two spots of blood. Then they drove to the village of Willis, as that is where the call had come from.

As they drove to Willis, the men saw a large dark spot in the road but did not stop to investigate. In Willis, they were told by Dexter that police in Belleville and Wayne had been called. They were also informed that Officers Krimmel and Erwin of the Michigan State Police were also working on the case.

Then Elliott, Klavitter and Oltersdorf began their ride back to the store, but this time, they stopped to investigate the dark spot in the road. The men found the spot with their flashlights and followed a trail of spots to the side of the road. There, they found Harry Cyb alive but unconsciousness. Cyb was rushed to Beyer Hospital in Ypsilanti, and the men waited to see if he would regain consciousness. After a time, the men returned to the store by Lincoln Consolidated School. Cyb never did regain consciousness and died at 9:30 in the morning.

The cause of Cyb's death was a blow to the head. Police later concluded that someone had struck Cyb over the head with a blunt object while he was pouring oil into the engine of a car. Then the suspects dragged the unconscious Cyb into the car and drove off with him.

When Elliott, Klavitter and Oltersdorf arrived at the store, they found Officer Erwin of the Michigan State Police there. Erwin had just taken Herman Crossie into custody. Erwin had been driving on Willis Road when he saw Crossie walking toward the area where the body of Cyb had been found. When Erwin slowed his car, Crossie paused, then went over to the car and told Erwin he was going to Ypsilanti. "You're crazy," said Erwin, and he told Crossie he was going in the wrong direction. Erwin told Crossie to get in the car and said he would give him a ride to Ypsilanti. As Crossie got in the car, Erwin noted that Crossie was partially intoxicated. Erwin also noted that Crossie had bloodstains on his right cheek and little finger. The stains appeared to Erwin to be about two hours old. Crossie's right hand also appeared to be hurt. When Erwin asked about his hand, Crossie said he had been cutting corn for his mother. Crossie added that he had cut twenty shocks. When asked about the blood on his clothing, Herman Crossie said he had been in a fight but did not say who with.

Herman Crossie was known to the police, as he had been arrested on June 3, 1924, for violating the Prohibition law. He was found guilty in circuit court and fined. He was also suspected of stealing chickens, but the evidence was insufficient.

Elliott left Crossie at the store in the custody of Oltersdorf and then went with Klavitter and Erwin to the Crossie home. There, they found Owen Lidke sitting in his car in front of the house. The officers found blood spots on Lidke's clothing. He was not intoxicated. The officers asked where William Crossie, the brother of Herman, was and were told he was in the house. At the house, a woman answered the door and asked what the officers wanted. A few seconds later, William Crossie came to the door, fully dressed and very drunk. The officers noted that there appeared to be bloodstains on his clothing.

When Crossie was asked where his car was, he said he did not know. He added that he had been driving. At this, it was pointed out that if he had been driving his car, he should know where it was. To this, Crossie said he would take them to the car. Crossie took the men to the car, which was in a ditch on the county line. Crossie sang all the way to the car. The officers found blood on the left fender and the left rear curtain of the car. There was wet sand on the running board as well. William explained that his brother Herman was driving when he went too far while trying to turn around and went into the ditch.

Then the officers drove Crossie—and most likely Lidke—to the store near Lincoln Consolidated School. William sang as they traveled down the road toward the school, but as they approached the spot where the body of Cyb was found, William stopped singing. He was quiet when they approached the site where the body was found. As the car was slowed when it neared the spot where the body of Cyb was found, Crossie all but stood up in his seat to look north, where the body had been left. Not once did any of the three men ask why they were being taken into custody. The three men, William and Herman Crossie and Owen Lidke, were housed in the Washtenaw County Jail.

The body of Harry Cyb was returned to the family home at the store, where it remained until Tuesday, September 22, 1925, when Cyb was buried

The Ypsilanti City Hall, in 1925, was located in the Second Empire–style house at 304 North Huron Street. The courtroom was on the second floor on the right. *Used with the permission of the Ypsilanti Historical Society.*

in St. John the Baptist Catholic Cemetery on River Street in Ypsilanti. Mary Cyb remained at the store for a time but realized she would be unable to continue the business, as she knew little English. Not long after the funeral, she began looking for someone who would rent or sell the store.

The examination of William and Herman Crossie and Owen Lidke, who were charged with the first-degree murder of Harry Cyb, opened before Justice D.Z. Curtiss in the municipal court of Ypsilanti on the evening of Thursday, October 1, 1925. The court was held in the City Hall of Ypsilanti, then in the Second Empire–style house at 304 North Huron Street. At least one thousand people crowded the lower floor of the building, filling the courtroom to capacity. Outside the building, people milled about yard.

A question that went about those gathered was: Will the Crossies get out of it? Those who lived in and around the village of Willis answered: "The law may let them out of it, but they won't get far."

The first official act of the proceedings was the censure of Luis Burk, the attorney for the Crossies, for being late. Justice Curtiss demanded the examination be conducted in a business-like manner.

The first witness called to testify was Mary Cyb, the widow of Harry. She spent an hour and a half answering questions asked in a language she could barely understand. Question by question, she retold the events of that night. "And so, she told her story, over and over again," noted the *Daily Ypsilanti Press* on Friday, October 2, 1925, "until at last all three attorneys were satisfied, and she was allowed to leave the witness stand to stand with the crowds along the wall for nearly another hour before the case was finally adjourned for the night." Her testimony was followed by others, including that of Undersheriff Dick Elliott.

The examination resumed the next afternoon, Friday, October 2, 1925, and again, many came to see the proceedings. The *Daily Ypsilanti Press*, on Saturday, October 3, 1925, reported:

> *The hall and rooms of the lower floor of the city hall, where the examination was held, was jammed with townspeople who crowded to hear what was being said and at the end fought to gain a glimpse of the accused men. Considerable difficulty was encountered by Justice Curtiss in quieting observers crowding the courtroom. By means of a step ladder, a group of boys unable to get within hearing in the crowded courtroom climbed to the sill of an outside window and watched the proceeding from there.*

At the start of the proceedings, Undersheriff Elliott was to be called to continue his testimony when Herbert W. Emerson of the University of Michigan arrived with the results of tests done on the stains that were found on the shirts of the accused men. The stains on the shirts where blood, according to Dr. Emerson. The stain on the fender of the car did not prove to be blood, but Dr. Emerson said he could not prove the stain was not blood. When Dr. Emerson was finished, Undersheriff Elliott resumed his testimony of the events of the night of the murder. He said he placed the shoe of Herman Crossie on a footprint that was found near the body of Cyb.

The shoe fit the print exactly, according to Elliott. The shoe, he continued, was tried in several of the footprints. None of the shoes of the officers would have fit the print, added Elliott.

The defense began the presentation of its case on Saturday, October 3, 1925, and called Florence Richardson to the stand. She had been riding in the front seat of a sedan as it turned the corner of the store and was within a few feet of the site of the attack. The *Daily Ypsilanti Press* reported on Monday, October 5, 1925:

> *She told how as she rode by, she saw a large open car standing at the filling station with Harry Cyb bending over the motor, as if to pour in oil. Outlined against the light of the gasoline pump, she saw the head and hand lifted as through to strike a blow of a man of small stature whom could not be recognized. The man was standing on the running board, leaning over Harry Cyb, she testified.*

The car, she said, had a dark-colored body, but she could not be sure of the color. "She was familiar with the Crossie car, she admitted, but she could not say that the car at the filling station was the same size," noted the account.

"I have known the Crossies for two or three years," testified Richardson, "and seen them often."

"Do you recognize any of these men as the man you saw at the filling station?" she was asked.

"No."

"Do you recognize anybody in the room as such?"

"No."

She had never seen Owen Lidke before the trial, she said.

The proceedings were concluded on the evening of October 8, 1925

"This case has been given an exhaustive inquiry," said Justice Curtiss. "The defendants have elected, as is their right, not to take the stand. The sheriff has made a thorough investigation, and the crime is still unsolved. There have been, to my mind, sufficient developments to indicate that these defendants might have committed this crime, and I am not willing to take the responsibility of dismissing the case but will hold the men to circuit court."

Rumors were going about Augusta Township by the end of January 1926 that Washtenaw County prosecutor William Laid was contemplating a motion of nolle prosequi—that is, not to proceed with the case. Laird, it was said, was reluctant to put the county through the expense of a trial, as he felt the evidence was insufficient for a conviction. The great weakness of the case was the inability of the prosecution to place the three accused men at the scene of the crime at the time it was committed. Witnesses who said the three were trying to pull their car out of a ditch at the time of the murder were questioned but would not change their stories.

A petition was circulated among the residents of Augusta Township requesting the assistance of Michigan attorney general Andrew B. Dougherty and was signed by over two hundred residents. The residents accused Laird of being lax in handling the case. A delegation of fourteen residents, including members of the township board, arrived in Lansing on Tuesday, February 2, 1926, to present the petition to Dougherty. The delegation did not meet with Dougherty, as he had unexpectedly been called away. Instead, the delegation had a meeting with a deputy. The delegation was assured by the deputy that a representative of the attorney general's department would be sent to Washtenaw County to investigate the case at once.

Assistant Attorney General Fred Warner arrived in Ann Arbor on Friday, February 5, 1926, to study all the facts concerning the case. Warner conferred with Laird and Undersheriff Dick Elliott and went over the stenographic reports of the preliminary hearing. He was informed of additional evidence that had been uncovered since the hearing. He also paid a visit to the scene of the crime. When he had completed his investigation, Warner returned to Lansing to make his report to Deputy Attorney General Clare Retan.

The attorney general could make one of three choices: He could order Laird to proceed with the case, send an attorney from his office in Lansing to prosecute the case in place of Laird or call for a one-man grand jury.

Laird received a letter from Retan on Friday, February 12, 1926, ordering him to proceed with the case. The letter informed Laird that the "attorney general's department has found there is reasonable cause to believe the prisoners are guilty, and the facts should be submitted to a jury as soon as possible."

Laird responded with a letter of his own on Saturday, February 13, 1926. Laird wrote:

> *In reference to your letter of February 11 regarding the above case, it appears that Mr. Warner has not reported to you the attitude of this office in respect to the trial of these men. I endeavored to make it plain to him at our conference last week that I did not believe the character of the evidence now available is sufficient to warrant a trial of these men at this time and*

that I would not try them until I am satisfied that we have enough facts to justify the submission of the same to a jury.

I have come to the conclusion after having spent the best part of the ten days immediately following the commission of the offense in investigating this case and after having personally examined all of the witnesses with but a few exceptions who had any knowledge bearing on the subject and with a full knowledge of all the facts which have been brought to light by reason of the investigation made. I have given this matter careful and deliberate consideration, and I feel that on account of the character of the evidence now available, I would not be justified in assuming the responsibility of asking the people of the county to stand the burden of such a trial at this time.

I also appreciate a certain amount of local prejudice and public hatred against the respondents has been voiced in one section of our county, but local prejudice is not proof of guilt, nor is public hatred a standard by which the innocence or guilt of an accused can be determined.

As I have already stated to Mr. Warner in view of the fact that your office is thoroughly familiar with the evidence and as you feel that under the circumstance these respondents should be tried immediately. I have no objection if your office wants to assume the responsibility of trying these men at this time. If you do, I am sure that the sheriff's department and the prosecutor's office will be glad to cooperate with you and will render every possible assistance.

In response to the letter, Dougherty sent a letter to Laird on Thursday, February 18, 1926, ordering him to proceed with the trial of the Crossies and Lidke or face proceedings to remove him from the office of prosecutor.

The prosecutor should not usurp the province of a jury. A conviction can very seldom be guaranteed, but that is no reason for not presenting proper cases to a jury for their determination. The duty of law enforcing officers to protect the lives and property of people in the state is greater than their duty to make a record for convictions.

We regret, therefore, that you assume the attitude you do but must insist on this case being brought to trial as soon as possible. Two of the respondents have already rested in jail several months. If all the facts are properly presented to a jury, we believe conviction may be secured.

Should you continue in your refusal to bring the case to trial, there is only one course left open to this department, and that is to make an application

to the governor for your removal from office. We trust it will not be necessary
for us to pursue that course.

Laird responded to Dougherty on February 19, 1926: "In view of the fact that you have assumed responsibility of insisting that the case against these men be brought on at once, the trial of the first of these respondents will begin upon the return of his counsel from California. I have been informed this will be in about ten days or two weeks."

As Laird believed he had the strongest case against Herman Crossie, he chose to prosecute him first. The trial was set for the March term.

There was keen interest in the case, most notably in Augusta Township, where many feared the Crossies and what might happen if they were released. Some who might have taken the stand against them were too frightened to do so. "A jury may free those men; perhaps the facts won't be strong enough to secure a conviction," said an unidentified resident of Augusta Township to the *Daily Ypsilanti Press* on Saturday February 20, 1926.

In that case, those of us who have been fighting for a trial can expect trouble
with them when they are released. We've all had trouble with them before.
Most of us think they are guilty; otherwise, we have gone to the trouble
of asking the state to prosecute the case when we understood the county
prosecutor was going to nolle posse it. But we aren't anxious to go through
Harry Cyb's experience.

Witnesses were called, including Robert Lord, who testified to the events of the night of the murder. The widow of Harry Cyb, who had moved to Detroit, returned to retell her version of that night. The officers who investigated the case recounted the events as well, much like they had at the preliminary hearing. Some of the witnesses could not be found for the trial, so their testimony from the preliminary hearing was read to the record.

The wife of William Crossie was called to the stand and told of the visit of Owen Lidke and Herman Crossie to the farm on the night Cyb was murdered. The men told her they were going to get beer and drove off in William's car. When the men returned, she said it was clear they had been drinking, as they were partly intoxicated. She said she was asleep when they returned and did not know the time this occurred.

The next witness was Owen Lidke. "As he experiences difficulty in hearing," reported the *Ypsilanti Daily Press* on Wednesday, March 17, 1926, "attorneys were obliged to stand over him and shout to make questions heard." Lidke said he had seen Herman Crossie before but did not know him. Herman asked Lidke to drive him to his mother's farm ten miles south of Ypsilanti. Lidke agreed. Lidke said his car failed to start when he tried to return to Ypsilanti. The Crossies suggested he go for a ride in their car. He said they left the farm around 7:25 p.m.

"Notwithstanding the fact that you wanted to be back in Ypsilanti at 6:30 p.m. and that you had not had your supper yet, you fooled around the yard for one hour, didn't you?" demanded Laird.

"Yes," answered Lidke. He went on to explain that he had a late lunch while still in Ypsilanti around 5:20 p.m.

William Crossie and Herman Crossie also took the stand, and all three told, for the most part, the same story. Before setting out, Herman and William had tried to talk Lidke into trading his 1925 Chevrolet for the Crossies' 1919 Buick. Lidke asked if the starter worked. William knew the starter had not worked for two weeks. He then tried to show that it did work. His attempt to prove it did work failed. Then Lidke admitted he did not hold title to his car, as it was partially owned by his brother. Then Lidke tried to start his car to go back to Ypsilanti, but it failed to start. This is when the Crossies suggested he join them in a ride.

William had wanted Herman to help him dig potatoes, but Herman wanted to go to Detroit. After some discussion, Herman agreed to help if William got them some beer. William said he knew of a place where they could get beer just over the line in Wayne County. Herman suggested they go there at once. Lidke was invited to join them. The three got in William's car and, after using the crank to start the motor, set out for the Blind Pig.

Lidke said it took them about a half hour to get there. "He told how they drove into the yard," reported the *Daily Ypsilanti Press* on Thursday, March 18, 1926, "and entered the kitchen of the house by a door on a porch. In the room were three young men, a small girl and an old woman, a Polish woman." Lidke said he had two bottles of beer and some hard liquor. He said he did not notice how many bottles of beer William had and did not know who paid for them.

Lidke said they left at about 10:00 p.m. After about five minutes, they realized they were on the wrong road. Herman, who was driving, in an effort to turn the car around, backed the car into a ditch. William began to bawl Herman out. "You're always picking on me," replied Herman. Then he struck the car with his fist.

Lidke said they were stuck in the ditch for about an hour. Then a farmer pulled the car out of the ditch with a stump puller. Then they pushed the car into a yard, as the clutch was out of order. A passing car gave the men a ride back to the Crossie farm.

Once they were back at the farm, Lidke went to work on his car. William and his wife wanted Lidke to help pay for the cost of repairing the car, which was stuck in the ditch. Lidke refused, and William and his wife took down his license plate number.

"Finally, the Crossies retired, leaving Lidke the lantern. Twice William came out to invite him to stay the night, but Lidke declined. After he had gone in for the last time, the officers arrived to arrest them," reported the *Daily Ypsilanti Press*'s account.

William Crossie was the next person called to the stand and confirmed the account testified by Lidke. Then Herman Crossie was called to the stand and told the same story as his brother William and Lidke. Herman said he was not walking the wrong way when he was picked up by Erwin and that Erwin was mistaken. The defense would point out that this was not the area Erwin usually patrolled, and he was mistaken about the direction. When asked why he stopped singing as he approached the site where Cyb's body was found, Herman said he stopped because of a hard look he was given by Officer Klavitter.

The defense rested, and the case went to the jury. Judge George Sample addressed them:

> This is a criminal case in which Herman Crossie, the respondent, is charged with the murder of Harry Cyb. It is claimed by the prosecution that although there were no eyewitnesses to the murder that, nevertheless, enough of facts and circumstances have been established to satisfy the members of the jury beyond a reasonable doubt as the guilt of the defendant.
>
> In criminal cases, there are two general classes of evidence: namely, direct evidence, which is evidence from eyewitnesses who claim to have seen the thing about which they testify….There is another class of evidence called circumstantial evidence, which is evidence of facts and circumstances which, when established, lead the mind to certain conclusions or inferences taken there from.

He reviewed the case for the prosecution.

Judge Sample defined first- and second-degree murder and manslaughter and told the jury they could find Herman Crossie guilty on one of these charges or find him innocent. He further reviewed the case for the defense.

The case went to the jury on Friday, March 19, 1926. When the jury retired that evening, they stood at six to six for conviction. They resumed deliberations the next morning and reached a unanimous decision, which was announced at 10:30 a.m. The verdict of the jury was that Crossie was not guilty. Herman Crossie was freed, and in time, the decision was made to not take William and Lidke to trial, and both were released.

That was where the matter rested—for a time.

Beatrice Sweet was nineteen years old in February 1931 and had been sentenced two years before for cashing a worthless check. She made a comment about her belief that she had been framed by a man named Grover Terry because she knew too much. That remark caused Washtenaw County deputy sheriff Lynn Squires to question her. She told Squires that she went to live in the home of Grover Terry in 1927 and learned that Terry had some part in a murder—the murder of Cyb. Sweet gave the officers the names of others who might tell what they knew. One of these people was Genevieve Allen, who was living with Fred Lagness at the time Cyb was murdered. Genevieve Allen married Lagness in January 1927, and in March, Lagness was sentenced to seven and half to fifteen years in Jackson Prison for armed robbery. (He had robbed a gasoline station on the corner of Ecorse and Telegraph Roads.)

Squires questioned those named by the women, including a Sumpter Township bootlegger and a gasoline station attendant. With the information provided, the officers were able to trace the steps of Lagness and Terry on the night of the murder.

Terry was arrested on suspicion of stealing chickens; he was convicted and sentenced to ninety days in jail. This allowed the officers to hold Terry as they proceeded to secure the last witnesses needed to convict him of murder. When confronted with the evidence, Terry confessed and named Lagness as the one who struck the fatal blow.

The men had stopped at the Cyb gasoline station sometime before the night of the murder and had seen Cyb with a thick roll of bills. On the night of September 18, 1925, the men decided to rob Cyb of his money. Lagness and Terry left the place in Dexter where Lagness and Allen were living and obtained liquor near Martinsville. They borrowed a hammer from Oliver Griffin's oil station in Sumpter Township. Terry stated in his confession:

We drove up to the gas station after dark—this was Cyb's gas station located at the corner of Willis and Whittaker Roads, Washtenaw County, Michigan. I was in the back seat at this time. Him and Fred had some argument over some liquor, the exact words I do not remember, when Fred hit him with a hammer or something and threw him in the front seat and got into the car and drove east on the Willis Road, and near a small bridge, Fred threw Cyb out of the car on the north side of the road. We then went and got some more liquor, then we went to my home south of Dexter Michigan on Fred Burch's farm.

Early on the morning of Monday, March 2, 1931, prosecuting attorney Albert J. Rapp, Deputy Sheriff Lynn Squires and Sergeant Bruce McGlone of the Michigan State Police left Ann Arbor and drove to Lansing. There, they obtained a temporary pardon for Lagness from Michigan governor Wilbur M. Brucker. From Lansing, the man went to the prison in Jackson and there, secured the release of Lagness. Then, with Lagness, they returned to Ann Arbor. There, Lagness made his confession to the murder of Harry Cyb.

Lagness, in his confession, named Terry as the killer of Cyb:

On the way over, when we turned onto the Willis Road, we planned to just drive in and get some oil and when he came out with the oil, we were going to stick him up. Well, he came out with the oil and put it in the car. When he bent over to put it in the car, Grove suggested that we would not stick him up because it would make too much noise with the pistol. So, while I was sitting at the wheel, he got out of the car with the hammer and hit Cyb over the head. Cyb fell down on the ground, and Grower picked him up and laid him on the front-left fender of the car. Then we drove down Willis Road with Cyb on the fender, and Terry Grower stood on the running board of the car and held him on. When we got down the about one-half mile, Terry lost hold of him and he [Cyb] fell off. After he fell off, I stopped the car, and Terry ran back to where Cyb was lying and went through his pockets. (I did not see this, but he told me.) Terry then shoved the body off the north side of the road and came back to the car. I did not see Terry hit but once, but he hit him harder than he intended to, and the other cuts and bruises must have happened when he fell off the car.

According to Lagness, all they got off Cyb was the ten-dollar bill they had given to him to pay for the oil and forty cents.

Grover Terry and Fred Lagness appeared before Circuit Court Judge George Sample on Tuesday, March 3, 1931. The two pleaded guilty and were sentenced to life imprisonment at Jackson.

Lagness, said Judge Sample, was one of the most hardened criminals he had ever interviewed. "He has no conscience for feelings of others as far as human beings are concerned." The *Washtenaw Tribune* reported on Wednesday, March 4, 1931, "Terry was ordered segregated at the prison on account of a disease which he is suffering,"

By this time, Mary Cyb had moved to Detroit, where she raised her five children. The grave of Harry Cyb is located at the rear of St. John the Baptist Catholic Cemetery on River Street in Ypsilanti. The headstone stands alone, as there appear to be no other graves near it.

11

NEW YORK OFFICER SHOT

A round 12:45 a.m. on Thursday, September 18, 1930, Peter J. O'Rourke was driving his car on Plymouth Road near Frains Lake. O'Rourke was a patrolman with the New York City Police Department. In the car with him were his wife and three daughters, Betty, ten years old; Marjorie, eight; and Gloria, seven. They were on the return trip from a vacation in Battle Creek.

As the family traveled on Plymouth Road, a second car, later described as a light coupe, pulled up beside them, and the occupants, without warning, opened fire on the O'Rourke car. Peter O'Rourke was struck and slumped over the steering wheel. His wife grabbed the emergency brake and stopped the car. The men in the coupe continued firing, sending some sixteen bullets into the car. In the car, ten-year-old Betty's head was grazed by a bullet, and Marjorie and Gloria were cut by flying glass.

"The two gunmen got out and came over to us." said Mrs. O'Rourke later. "I told them all we had was fifty dollars and that we were on our way home. They refused the money and said, 'You better drive your husband to University Hospital in Ann Arbor.' Then they drove off....I took the wheel and drove to Ann Arbor and took my husband to the hospital. I was slightly cut by flying glass."

"Two wounds appear on the face of the patrolman, one below each eye, but it could not be definitely stated at the hospital whether they were caused by one or two bullets," reported the *Ypsilanti Daily Press*. At this time, his condition was described as "fair." Doctors said it was most likely O'Rourke would be blind if he recovered.

Earlier in the evening, Miss Dorothy Strout was driving on the same road with M.W. Shellman when a light coupe drove up beside them. One of the occupants of the car shouted something that sounded like, "Get over!" She increased her speed and left the light coupe behind. Three shots were then fired into her car, and if any one of the shots had penetrated through the back seat, a fatality would have resulted. The account from the *Ypsilanti Daily Press* of Thursday, September 18, 1930, reported:

> *Miss Strout stopped when the firing commenced, and one of the bandits jumped into her car and, holding a gun on the couple, forced them to drive into a side road, where he robbed Mr. Shellman of ten dollars. Miss Strout, who was wearing a valuable diamond ring, slipped it from her finger and placed it in her shoe, thus retaining possession of it. When the thug was leaving the machine, Mr. Shellman protested that they had some distance to go and that their gasoline was low. The bandit returned them one dollar. The couple stated that they were treated considerately by the man who stepped into the car.*

About ten minutes later, a car driven by a Frank Novotney stopped when menaced by armed men in a car. One of the men climbed into the car and directed Mr. Novotney to move the car to the side of the road. In the car with Mr. Novotney were his wife and two other women, all from Chicago. The *Ypsilanti Daily Press* reported on September 18, 1930:

> *After a methodical search, which delayed the party for about ten minutes, he allowed them to go without having found any valuables. While in the car, he kept his gun pointed at Mr. Novotney....All members of the party asserted this morning that they had been treated kindly by the robber. They described one as blond and tall and the other darker and shorter in stature....They said the men who held them up were from eighteen to twenty years old and appeared to be "nice boys."...They described both as slim.*

As soon as word of the shootings and holdup reached police, patrols were dispatched to Plymouth Road and began searching for the gunmen. Two men found sleeping in a car within a few miles of the scene of the shooting were taken into custody but were later released. Four other suspects were later taken into custody but were released.

Two weeks later, the comparison of fingerprints from the Shellman car identified Russell McComis, seventeen, and William Brown, twenty-one, both from Detroit, as the men who had shot O'Rourke. The two men matched the description of the men given by witnesses. Information of the two were sent nationwide by Wayne County sheriff Ira Wilson. "The pair," reported the *Ypsilanti Daily Press* on Wednesday, October 1, 1930, "is well known to Wayne officers, and both are ex-convicts. Both are known dope fiends."

Patrolman Richard Holdburg of the Port Huron Police Department found two young men loitering in a car near a gas station. One of these men was Russell McComis, and the other was Russell McCommis, twenty-one, of Detroit. Officer Holdburg searched the two and took a revolver from each of them. He placed the two under arrest and handcuffed them together. Holdburg then called for a police flyer.

Responding to the call were Sergeant Roy Shambleau and Lieutenant Thomas Hastings. McComis and McCommis were placed in the car and began the trip to the station. Holdburg followed behind in the car the two had been loitering in. "At Maple and State streets the police flyer suddenly swerved to the curb, and Holdburg heard shots. As he sped toward the corner, he saw the handcuffed prisoners leap from the flyer," reported the *Detroit Times* on Saturday, October 11, 1930.

McComis had a pistol strapped to the small of his back and had managed to work it free. He shot Shambleau, who was driving, and he slumped forward, dead. Then McComis shot Hastings in the hand as the two struggled for the gun. McComis and McCommis rushed from the car and, still handcuffed together at the wrist, began running through an alley. Holdburg jumped from the car he was driving and gave chase. McComis and McCommis continued running and tried to pass a tree, one on the left and the other on the right. The tree between them brought the two to a sudden stop. Holdburg fired twice at the two, the bullets striking the tree close to their heads. The two offered no resistance when Holdburg caught up with them, McComis having dropped his gun as he was running.

"I knew we were on the police circulars for some jobs we pulled," said McComis. "We were certain to be identified and sent up if they took us to headquarters. I decided to try a getaway....When the officer that arrested me searched McCommis and me, he didn't catch my gun which I had tucked down in the back of my trousers," said McComis. "After we had gone a little ways, I managed to get the gun out and fired three times."

For the two weeks prior, the pair had been staying in a cottage on a lake. That Saturday night, the two and two companions moved into an apartment in Port Huron. From the apartment, McComis and McCommis set out for a place to rob. "We were broke and had nothing to eat," said McCommis, "so we started out to find a gas station that looked good."

When police searched the apartment where the two had been staying, they found William Brown and Charlotte Rawless, a seventeen-year-old girl from Clearfield, Pennsylvania. The two were taken into custody. The Rawless girl was described as the sweetheart of McComis.

On Saturday, October 11, McComis entered a plea of guilty for the murder of Shambleau before the justice court. He was then rushed to the circuit court, where Judge William Robertson was waiting. There was reason for the rush, as one thousand people were milling around the courthouse. Several hundred people forced their way into the courtroom. "Police, fearing some untoward circumstance might rouse the mob to violence, moved about, cautioning citizens against any demonstration," reported the *Detroit Times* on Sunday, October 12, 1930. McComis was sentenced to life imprisonment in solitary confinement and hard labor.

After the trial, McComis was allowed a brief moment with his sweetheart, Charlotte Rawless, who was being held for investigation. He, she said, was her first true love. "Well, kid," he said, "I'll be gone a long time. I'll be gone sixteen years at least." "I'll wait," promised Charlotte. Then they kissed each other goodbye. Police had to pull the two apart.

McComis was then surrendered to a detachment of the Michigan State Police, who formed a square around him and moved him to a car before the crowd knew what was happening. He was delivered to Jackson Prison four hours later, just eighteen hours after the murder of Shambleau.

McCommis was sent to Ohio to face charges of murder in the first degree. William Brown was turned over to deputies of the Washtenaw County Sheriff's Department and taken to the jail in Ann Arbor. There, he faced charges of shooting Peter O'Rourke.

Late on the night of Sunday, October 26, 1931, the Washtenaw County Sheriff's Department received a call from a telephone operator who informed the officers that she had been told someone was trying to get into the second house east of Milan Road. This may have reminded the deputies of a number of calls they had received the night before from someone who said they needed help. The person called back a number of times to ask if the men had been sent out. The call for aid was fake and left deputies puzzled.

In response to this call, two deputies, James Wanseck and Alex Schlupe, left the jail to investigate. This left Deputy William Dailey as the only man on duty at the jail. The jail was never left unmanned. Around 12:15 on

Monday morning, someone knocked on the door at the jail. Officer Dailey, from inside the building, asked the person outside what they wanted. He was told the person was in need of a place to spend the night. (Jails will sometimes take in persons who have no place to go.) Dailey opened the door, and the man rammed a gun into his side and demanded the keys to the cell block. Dailey told the man he could find the keys in the drawer of the desk near the door. The man then used his gun as a club and struck Daily across the bridge of his nose. Then the man stepped behind the desk to search for the keys. The *Ypsilanti Daily Press* reported:

> *As he lowered his head slightly while attempting to locate them, Deputy Dailey sprang at him, and the two fought for possession of the bandit's gun. In the course of the struggle, the stranger kicked the deputy, fracturing two ribs, and then ran for the back door of the office, which opens into a court way where a machine was waiting. As he reached the door, he fired at the officer, who returned the shots. He is believed to have escaped in a car which garage employees across the road had noticed parked there. They also noticed that the car lights were used as signals.*
>
> *Deputy Sheriff Jacob Andres, who maintains his residence at the jail, heard the shots and rushed to the office while Mrs. Andres phoned the police department from an extension telephone. When Deputy Andres arrived, he found the other officer on the floor covered with blood.*

A search for the attacker was unsuccessful. Deputy Dailey was taken to University Hospital and released the same day.

Deputies Wanzeck and Schlupe were back at the jail by 12:35 a.m., having found that they had been called out on a false call. A search of the jail found William Brown in his cell fully dressed, as if he was expecting to leave soon. Brown admitted that there was a plan to free him from the jail.

That same morning, Brown pleaded guilty to the charge of armed robbery and was sentenced to Jackson Prison "for the rest of his natural life."

As Brown was facing the court, Peter O'Rourke was leaving Ann Arbor to return to New York. There was a slight chance he could regain some sight in one eye.

A search of the jail uncovered hacksaw blades in the possession of Fred Cameron, who admitted the blades were intended for Brown. A woman had been caught talking to Cameron sometime before the attempt to free Brown. From the woman, Cameron passed a message to Brown, that he was to be freed that Saturday or Sunday night. The woman was Elsa Lutz, the twenty-four-year-old sister of Brown. She, with Irene Brown, the eighteen-year-old wife of Brown, were taken into custody that day in Detroit and sent to the jail in Ann Arbor.

The women were taken into custody at the same time as Clyde "Tony" Pyle, who was identified that evening by Deputy Sheriff Dailey as the man who assaulted him. Pyle denied taking part in the attempt until the afternoon of Thursday, October 30, when he broke down under questioning by Deputy Sheriff Dailey. The *Ypsilanti Daily Press* reported:

> The confession…told briefly of how the prisoner had sought shelter for the night at the jail, covered the deputy with his gun and fumbled in the drawer of the desk for the keys of the lower cell block. He admitted struggling for possession of the weapon with Dailey and told of how he managed to unbolt the back door when the two rolled over there. At the door, he said the gun he carried was discharged.

Pyle said Lutz offered him $200 to try to free Brown and $500 if he succeeded in releasing him. William Brown, in Jackson Prison, also made a confession that day. Pyle, for his efforts, was sentenced to life in prison.

Peter O'Rourke died at the age of fifty-seven, on March 12, 1954. His obituary in the *New York Times* noted he "died of a heart attack while dancing with his wife, Alice, at a party at the Lighthouse, the New York Association for the Blind."

12

McHENRY KILLINGS

E mmett Gill held the office of Washtenaw County clerk from 1935 to 1939. At the end of each working day, Gill would leave his office in Ann Arbor and drive to his home in Dixboro. As he was making the drive home on the evening of Thursday, September 30, 1937, he noticed a car parked by the roadside near the east entrance of Arbor Crest Cemetery on Plymouth Road. He gave little thought to the car, as there was nothing unusual about its appearance.

The next morning, on Friday, October 1, 1937, as Gill was driving to Ann Arbor, he again noticed the car still parked by the roadside. After he arrived at his office, he informed Washtenaw County sheriff Jacob Andres of the abandoned vehicle.

A deputy was sent to investigate but was unable to examine the inside of the car, as the doors were locked. Looking in the car, he could see blankets piled on the front passenger seat and on the back seat. The car was towed to a garage in Ann Arbor. There, Sheriff Andres forced open the front door of the sedan. He saw the front passenger seat was covered with blankets and pillows. When Sheriff Andres lifted the blankets from the front seat, he uncovered the body of a woman. He ordered the car be returned to where it had been found. As this was being done, the coroner, Dr. Edwin Ganzhorn and Prosecutor Albert Rapp were informed of the find. Once the car was back where it had been found, Dr. Ganzhorn began his examination of the body. At the same time, Sheriff Andres lifted the blankets from the floor of the rear seat. There, he uncovered the body of a boy.

The woman was identified as Adele McHenry, fifty-five years of age, from her clothing, jewelry and papers in her purse. The body of the boy was her seven-year-old son, James McHenry Jr.

Having completed the preliminary examination of the bodies in the car, Dr. Ganzhorn had them removed and taken to the Staffer Funeral Home in Ann Arbor. This was where the autopsies were performed.

Investigators checked the license plate number of the car and learned it was registered to James G. McHenry, a prominent Detroit attorney. The family lived in an apartment in Detroit and had a farm south of the city of Ypsilanti, as well as a house in the city of Ypsilanti. When Mr. McHenry was contacted by police in Detroit, he informed them that he had been searching for his wife since the previous evening. He had to tell her that their twenty-three-year-old daughter, Ruth, had killed herself. When McHenry was told that his wife and son were dead, he responded, "Well, I'll be darned." He set out at once for Ann Arbor.

In 1937, Ruth McHenry was a troubled young woman. Her father informed Sheriff Andres that she had been diagnosed with dementia praecox. Today, she would have been diagnosed with schizophrenia. As a child, Ruth had attended a private school for girls in Detroit and graduated high school from a fashionable school for girls in Maryland. "When she was seventeen," explained her father, "she began to get moody and despondent. She didn't do anything violent, she just acted strangely."

"I have expected something like this to happen for some time," said her older sister Marie Isabella, a twenty-seven-year-old student at the University of Michigan School of Law. "She felt the whole family was against her. She had been morose and moody for some time."

"Ruth," added Marie Isabella, "was given to long periods of being depressed. She was gloomy and despondent at these times. Ruth wouldn't speak to the family."

The family placed Ruth under the care of Dr. Leo Bartemeir, who diagnosed her. Her treatment continued with an appointment at his office in the General Motors Building in Detroit every Thursday. For the previous three months Ruth had been staying at the home of Edward B. Green, a professor of psychology at the University of Michigan. He and his wife, Katherine, also a psychologist, ran a nursery out of their home in Ann Arbor. "Ruth had shown a marked improvement while she was at the Greens'," said her sister Marie Isabella. "We thought they were helping her a lot," continued Marie Isabella. "They gave her things to do about the house. They had children there in the nursery school, and Ruth always liked children."

Virginia Johnston, a twenty-two-year-old psychologist who was employed by the Greens and was a friend of Ruth, described Ruth as retiring and inclined to melancholia. She added that Ruth was "badly adjusted to life" and had no close boyfriends. Ruth, noted Johnston, did not speak to many people.

On Tuesday, September 28, 1937, Ruth left the Green home without permission and made her way to Detroit. Once in Detroit, she went to a major department store. At the store, she expressed an interest in purchasing a coat. An employee of the store called her father to ask if he would approve the charge. "The store phoned me and asked if I would approve of my daughter charging a coat for $23.00," explained Mr. McHenry, "I approved it." Once the charge was approved, Ruth canceled her order for the coat. She then went to the sporting goods department and, with the charge, purchased a .22-caliber rifle for $22.50 and a box of cartridges for $0.40.

Then Ruth returned to the Green home in Ann Arbor, arriving there around 9:00 p.m. She gave no reason for her absence. No one had seen her carry the rifle into the house and to her room on the second floor. She may have been able to conceal the rifle because of the placement of the stairs in the house.

Adele McHenry, the mother of Ruth, had been staying at the family's summer home at Ypsilanti with her seven-year-old son, James Jr. At about 8:30 a.m. on Thursday, September 30, 1937, Adele called the Green home. "I am going to take Ruth to the doctor in Detroit," she said, "and I will keep her there for a couple of days" It was her practice to take Ruth to Detroit every Thursday for her appointment with Dr. Baterneir. James Jr. was to go with them to Detroit, as he was to have his tonsils removed Friday morning at Harper Hospital.

Around 9:45 a.m., Amanda Russ, a maid employed by the Greens, saw James Jr. playing on the lawn of the Green house as Adele sat behind the wheel of the car. Ruth came out of the house wearing a coat and holding a number of bundles in her arms. The bundles, Russ said later, were too small to have concealed a rifle. Ruth may have hidden the rifle under her coat. Russ watched as Ruth and James Jr. got in the back seat of the car. Then the three set off for Detroit.

"The mother was evidently driving," said Sheriff Andres later. "Ruth was probably in the back seat with Jimmy. He must have been asleep because his shoes were off when his body was found. During the drive, Ruth fired rifle shots into the back of her mother's head, then killed her brother." Ruth fired three shots into the back of her mother's head. James Jr. was shot six times in the back of the head and once behind his left eye. His skull had two fractures, as if he was struck with a blunt object.

Ruth pushed the body of her mother to the right corner of the front seat and covered it over with blankets. Adele had been taking the blankets from the summer home to the family apartment in Detroit. Then Ruth moved the body of James Jr. to the floor of the rear seat and covered it with blankets. After this, Ruth got in the driver's seat, and started off, but because she was unfamiliar with driving a car, she stalled it near Arbor Crest Cemetery.

Two women who lived near the site later told investigators about a young woman who asked for help starting a stalled car. The two women said the young woman was nervous. The two told her they were unable to help start a stalled car. At this, the young woman ran off. The young woman matched the description of Ruth.

Somehow, Ruth was able to make her way to Detroit while carrying the rifle. She may have hitchhiked. Around 4:00 p.m., Ruth arrived at her family's home, a second-floor apartment at 296 East Kirby Avenue. She asked William Hondorf, a handyman, to open the basement door to the building. She then asked Hondorf to leave the door open for an hour. Hondorf later said Ruth had nothing in her hands but her purse. He also said she was excited and appeared to have been crying.

Ruth had most likely hidden the rifle nearby and retrieved it after Hondorf had left. Inside the apartment, she waited for her fourteen-year-old brother, Donald, to return home. Donald was a student at the Detroit University School, a private school located at Mack Avenue and Cook Road. He arrived home at 5:30 p.m. Donald said, "The house was dark, all the window shades pulled down and the doors locked. I finally went to the front door and tried again to get it open. As I grabbed the door handle, I heard a shot. The bullet came through the curtain on the door, smashed the glass and hit me in the forehead. It just missed my spectacles." Donald received only a slight wound to the scalp. "I ran to the home of a neighbor, Frank Weber, and he called the police."

Police entered the apartment through the kitchen door to find Ruth on the living room floor, alive but unconscious, a bullet wound to her head. She died a few hours later at Harper Hospital.

Funeral services were held for the three on October 4, 1937. All three were buried in the same lot at Highland Cemetery in Ypsilanti. The surviving members of the family agreed: Ruth "did not know what she was doing."

James McHenry continued to practice law until his death at the age of ninety-one on August 12, 1963. He rests between his wife, Adele, and his daughter Ruth.

The majority of those who suffer from metal illness have no desire to harm others and wish to be left alone. The number of those who do have violent tendencies tend to be self-destructive and pose a risk to themselves, not to others. Those who are a risk to others are the rare exception.

13

ELEANOR FARVER MURDER

THE SEARCH FOR THE MAN WHO DID NOT EXIST

Eleanor Farver was, on Tuesday, September 22, 1970, a forty-six-year-old, twice-divorced mother of six living at 2931 Joy Road near Pontiac Trail. This was a former one-room schoolhouse that had been converted into living quarters. Farver had been in a relationship with a man she knew as John Burns. He was sixty-two years of age but looked forty-five. He had been a frequent visitor to the home, but two weeks before, Farver told Burns that she wished to end the friendship, as she had discovered Burns was married.

That afternoon, Farver went into a pump house, a lean-to building attached to the house, to check on chicken eggs that were being hatched in an incubator. "A witness peering out a window of the dwelling told deputies she saw Burns suddenly appear at the side of the house, raise a shotgun to his shoulder and point it into the doorway of the pump house, authorities reported. Three gunshot reports were heard moments later," reported the *Ann Arbor News* on September 23, 1970.

The occupants of the house rushed outside to find Farver on the pump house floor. She had been struck once in the stomach and once in the head. She apparently died almost immediately. The third shot, fired from about three feet away, had missed. Those who had been in the house did not see where Burns had gone. "Sheriff's uniformed sergeant Richard Sober, the first officer on the scene, found a woman relative of Mrs. Farver carrying a shotgun through the house, and when he ordered her to come outside, she emerged weeping and in hysterics. The woman said she had the gun to protect herself after finding Mrs. Farver," noted the *Ann Arbor News*.

A search for Burns began almost immediately, but no trace of him was found. Three shotgun shells were found at the scene. The next morning, Wednesday, September 23, 1970, two detectives from the sheriff's office searched the Oakland-Washtenaw County line area in a helicopter. At the same time, a dozen officers on foot and in scout cars combed the woods and gravel pits near South Lyon. "We have no indication that Burns has fled the state or even this area," said Washtenaw County sheriff Douglas Harvey. "Without such an indication, we're moving on the assumption he is still around."

The search continued on Thursday, September 24, 1970, with two detectives in a helicopter cruising over parts of Salem Township and Livingston and Oakland Counties. "Beneath them, squads of sheriff's deputies searched abandoned farms, gravel pits and country lanes in an attempt to locate Burns's 1960 blue Chevrolet station wagon. But the daylong dragnet produced nothing," reported the *Ann Arbor News* on September 25, 1970.

Detectives were correct in their assumption that Burns was hiding in the area. After the murder, he had hidden himself in a hay barn across Joy Road from the murder scene. There, he had made a room for himself out of bales of hay. This room was about twenty-five feet above the floor and was reachable by climbing the bales of hay. The barn could be seen from the scene of the murder. And from the barn, Burns could have seen the pump house where Farver had died.

During his time hiding in the barn, Burns had written on the wall of the barn an admission to the murder in crayon. The admission read: "I was here ten days and nights. I could have killed the son many times from here. He was a skunk. Year 1970 [ninth month]. I shot and killed the woman I loved, Eleanor Farver….I was being made a fool. I rather see her dead than for another [to] have her. The son helped put his mother where she lies today. I myself will be dead when this is discovered." The admission was found during a search of the barn after empty food cans were found in the area.

On November 12, 1970, Anna, the wife of Burns who was living in South Lyon, received a five-page letter from her husband that had been mailed from Northville, about ten miles to the southeast of South Lyon. "In the first part of the letter," reported the *Ann Arbor News* on November 13, 1970, "the officers said he admitted killing Mrs. Farver and said it was an accident, but in the latter portion, he wrote that the victim 'deserved' to die. The letter bore dirt marks, the officers said."

Burns had remained in the barn for about ten days, detectives concluded, and then convinced a Washtenaw County farmer he had known for some time that he was "an innocent victim of circumstances." The farmer had taken Burns in and hidden him in his home. Soon after, the farmer drove Burns to the main bus terminal in Detroit. There, the farmer purchased a ticket to Altoona, Pennsylvania, for Burns. The farmer watched as Burns boarded the bus. Once in Altoona, Burns got in touch with a friend, who loaned him several hundred dollars. Then Burns traveled to Cheyenne, Wyoming, which was said to have been his childhood home. After a few days, Burns continued on to Houston, Texas. From there, all trace of him was lost.

"In homicide investigations where the suspect is known but cannot be found, a common investigation technique is to explore the suspect's background. Bits and pieces of knowledge about a person's past behavior can frequently become clues to future actions," noted the *Ann Arbor News* on June 20, 1983. In this case, detectives learned the suspect they were seeking, John Edward Burns, did not and had never existed. The man who called himself John Edward Burns had arrived in South Lyon in Oakland County in 1947 and had worked as a manual laborer on farms in western Wayne County and eastern Washtenaw County. He found employment as a janitor at a school in South Lyon, where he was said to be well liked. Every year on the day school pictures were to be taken for the yearbook, he was always absent. Those who knew him said he was a loner and was into physical fitness and health foods. This was a man, it was said, who was self-sufficient and could live off the land. He was a trapper and a hunter. He dressed in western-style clothing—cowboy boots, big belt buckles and jeans—long before it was fashionable.

Being careful to cover his past, Burns gave different dates of birth when applying for a driver's license, an insurance policy and his social security number, as well as his marriage license. Along with giving a different date of birth, each time, he gave a different place of birth—Pennsylvania, Montana and Missouri—in any one of four years. His wife never met any of his relations, and after all those years, there was only one photograph taken of him. Clearly, this was a man who was hiding from something in his past.

When there were no more leads to follow, the case turned cold, but it was not forgotten.

William Eskridge joined the Washtenaw County Sheriff's Department in 1975, five years after the Eleanor Farver murder. That same day, he was assigned the investigation. He kept the file in his desk and worked the investigation at every opportunity. All he needed was the right tip.

The right tip came in when the murder of Eleanor Farver was depicted on the television show *Unsolved Mysteries*, hosted by actor Robert Stack. After the broadcast, several people called police to say Burns was living near Altoona, Pennsylvania. There, Burns was living in a two-room log cabin on a wooded rural route. Detective Eskridge traveled to Pennsylvania and, with Altoona police and the state police, placed Burns under surveillance. Neighbors, in cooperation with police, called Burns on the telephone and asked him over to their house. As he stepped out of his cabin at 6:00 p.m., he was surrounded by eleven law enforcement officers dressed in camouflage outfits. At first, Burns refused to believe they were police and demanded to see a badge. Then he admitted to the killing of Eleanor Farver but insisted it was an accident. Further, he said, Farver was the only woman he had ever loved.

Burns had been living under the name Steven Edward Vance. His real name was Wilford Paul Cashman. Cashman, detectives learned, had escaped from a Pennsylvania prison exercise yard at 3:30 p.m. on August 15, 1947, after he had served less than four years of a four-to-fourteen-year sentence. He had been convicted of burglary, larceny, receiving stolen goods, forgery, assault and battery, assault with intent to ravish and statutory rape.

Cashman had settled near Altoona, where he did off jobs, about seven years after the Farver murder. There, he was described as a "deeply religious man who loved kids, loved animals and was friendly with everyone." The *Ann Arbor News* reported on June 3, 1987, "Cashman built the cabin he lived in on a mountain in the Allegheny Range near Altoona, sided it in stones, built a stone fireplace, installed plumbing, dug and pumped his own reservoir and strung wires from the cabin to the home of his nearest neighbor a quarter-mile away for electricity."

Vance was the first name of Farver's adult son, who hated the man he had known as Burns, and in return, Burns hated the son. "Vance, the son, is even said to have bragged to family and friends over the years that he murdered Cashman and burned his body," noted the *Ann Arbor News* on June 3, 1987.

Cashman did not fight extradition to Michigan, explaining, "I'm too old, I's sick, I'm tired and I want to get it over with." He was returned to Michigan, and the preliminary court hearing to determine if there was sufficient evidence against Cashman for a trial, was held on Monday, August 17, 1987, Judge Karl V. Fink presiding.

"I saw him load the shells into the shotgun," testified Melody Taylor, Farver's daughter-in-law. But she said she did not see Cashman fire the gun. She said that about ten days before the murder, she and Farver were driving home when Cashman saw them. He wheeled his truck around and followed them to the house. "Eleanor jumped out of the car," said Taylor, "and closed the gate, and that's when he drove up. He jumped out and stood on the running board of his truck and shouted and waved his arms. He was holding what looked like dynamite. He said he would blow us all to hell. There was a lot of cussing and swearing…all of it was directed at Eleanor." Taylor said Farver had been dating Cashman for almost a year. The two had talked about getting married and had taken the blood test that was required before obtaining a marriage license. Farver ended the relationship after learning that Cashman was married.

Another witness was Nina, the twenty-six-year-old daughter of Farver who was nine at the time of the shooting. She was home from school that day, recovering from an appendectomy. "I saw him," said Nina, "and ran to the dining room to tell Melody he was there and that he was carrying a gun. I didn't have time to tell her before we heard the shots. It was two quick shots, a very brief pause, then another shot."

Dr. Robert Hendricks, the Washtenaw County medical examiner, told the court that Farver was killed by two shotgun blasts. One shot, he said, was to the head, and the other was to the stomach.

Lloyd Powell, the chief county public defender, asked Judge Fink to reduce the charge against Cashman to "no more than involuntary manslaughter," as there had been no intent to kill Farver. Judge Fink concluded, that "it does appear the defendant with a deadly weapon went to the victim's home after on a previous occasion having made serious threats. He loaded the gun and fired three shots. That certainly was no accident. A murder has been committed." Judge Fink ordered Cashman be bound over for trial.

The case came to trial in late November 1987. At the trial, Melody Taylor and Nina Farver repeated their testimonies from the preliminary examination. Additional testimonies were provided by Robert Potts, a nephew of Farver who was visiting that day.

"I seen him raise the shotgun and pull the trigger," said Potts.

"You saw him pull the trigger?" asked Prosecution Attorney William Delhey.

Firmly, Potts answered, "Yes."

Dr. Robert Hendrix told the court that Farver had died from a shotgun blast to the head. The second wound to the abdomen may have proven fatal if not treated in time. He further said that there were no powder burns on the body, indicating the shots were fired from more than four or five feet away from Farver.

Detective William Eskridge told the court about the arrest of Cashman. "I asked him if he had killed Eleanor Farver, and he said, 'Yes, but it was an accident.'…He said she grabbed the end of the gun barrel, and it went off. I asked him if he could explain how [the gun] went off three times, and he didn't say anything."

Cashman testified in his own defense and told his version of events. "Much of Cashman's testimony was delivered in a faltering voice, sometimes interrupted by sobs, forcing jurors and others to strain to understand him. Judge Ross W. Campbell told the defendant, 'I'm six feet away, and I can't hear you,'" noted the *Ann Arbor News* on December 1, 1987.

Public Defender Powell asked Cashman, "Wilford, do you still love Eleanor Farver?"

Cashman answered, "I love her very much."

"Did you intend to kill her?" asked Powell.

"No," answered Cashman, "I didn't kill her. The gun shot her. I didn't."

Cashman said he had purchased a new semiautomatic shotgun from a man he knew only as "Ben" and was planning to go hunting that day. He stopped by the house and was talking to Farver about the two of them taking a trip together to Pennsylvania. "I went to bring the gun up over my shoulder. It got up about waist high, and it went off." He said he tried to help Farver, but as he did, Farver grabbed the end of the gun, and it went off, hitting her in the head. Cashman admitted to writing the confession on the wall of the barn but explained, "That's not exactly what I wanted to say. I didn't want her dead."

Soon after the shooting, Cashman said, he traded the gun with a man he met in the woods. He did not know the man who, according to Cashman, told him the gun had a defective safety catch and a hair trigger.

When questioned about the incident that occurred ten days before the shooting, when Cashman waved what appeared to be dynamite and said he "would blow them all to hell," Cashman said, "She was mistaken." He explained that he wanted Farver's son Vance and his family to move out of the house. He said he was waving red candles that looked like dynamite. He called it an "innocent threat."

In his closing arguments, Prosecuting Attorney William Delhey called on the jury to find Cashman guilty of first-degree murder, as Delhey said, the evidence clearly showed he went to the house to kill Farver. "A [semiautomatic-loading shotgun] doesn't fire like a machine gun. It fires each time you pull the trigger, which is a willful, deliberate act." Delhey further stated that Cashman's guilt was proven by the fact he fled the scene after the shooting. He called this "guilt by flight—he left the scene. If this was an accident, would he have left the scene?" After all, Delhey pointed out, if this was an accident, why didn't Cashman seek help for the woman he loved?

The jury found Cashman guilty of second-degree murder. Cashman was scheduled to be sentenced on January 28, 1988, but he never heard his sentence pronounced. He died of heart trouble on the evening of January 7, 1988.

14

KENSLER MURDER AT MANCHESTER

After Peter Kensler's murder, it seemed like everyone who had known him had something nice to say about him. He was said to have been a friendly man, willing to help others. He was a man, it was said, who did not have an enemy in the world. Well, is appears he did have at least one enemy. His life, it seems, was more complicated than those who knew him realized.

Peter A. Kensler was born in Manchester on May 21, 1939, the son of Craig and Louise Kensler. Peter Kensler graduated from Manchester High School in 1957 and received his bachelor's degree from the University of Michigan in 1961 and his law degree from the University of Detroit Law School in 1966. From 1968 to January 1974, he had been a partner in a law firm at Manchester with James Hensley.

Kensler left the partnership to open his own office. There may have been some animosity between Hensley and Kensler at the time, as Hensley filed suit against Kensler, and Kensler responded by filing suit against Hensley. The suits were ordered to be suppressed by a judge of the Washtenaw County Court so that only the attorneys involved could examine files. These files have never been made public.

On January 27, 1976, Kensler was elected to the board of directors of the Union Savings Bank of Manchester. This was the result of a proxy fight among shareholders, resulting in the removal of the president, chairman and all but one of the board members. Kensler, it was reported later, had played only a minor role in the takeover and had attended only two of the meetings of the shareholders who were planning the proxy fight. His former law partner, Hendley, had been a chairman of the board until the year before. "I kind of got myself removed from the situation," said Hendley in an interview held before the murder. "I just decided that after thirty-six years, it was time to retire. If I didn't do it then, I might never have done it! I was not voted off."

In 1976, Peter Kensler was a thirty-six-year-old bachelor who, for the previous seven years, had lived alone in a ranch-style house at 17750 Sharon Valley Road in Sharon Township. The house was located on a ten-acre site set off from the road at the end of a long driveway. He called his home Walnut Grove because of the nearby walnut trees.

Based on the available evidence, investigators concluded that Kensler was alone in his house on Tuesday, February 4, 1976. Around 5:00 p.m. Kensler may have seen a vehicle, possibly a station wagon, coming up the long driveway to the house. He may have known who was in the vehicle and put on a three-quarter-length coat before going outside. There may have been two men in the vehicle. After the vehicle came to a stop, a man got out and perhaps exchanged words with Kensler. Then the man leveled a 20-gauge shotgun at Kensler. Kensler made a run for the house.

The man fired the shotgun at Kensler but missed. Then the man fired again, this time hitting Kensler in the left shoulder, causing him to spin around and fall to the ground. As Kensler lay face-up on the ground, the man stood over him and fired a round into his face. Then the man fired a second round into Kensler's face. After this, the man returned to the vehicle, got back in and drove back down the driveway to the road.

When Kensler failed to arrive for an appointment at his office the next morning, his law office secretary, Sandra Retzlaff, became concerned. She called the Kensler house on the phone but received no answer. As the calls to the house proved futile, Retzlaff called Peter's sister, Pat Fitzgerald. The two went to the house, arriving around 12:30 p.m. After finding his body, they called police.

For a criminal investigation to be successful, it is imperative for the crime scene to be preserved so evidence can be recovered. By the time detectives arrived at the Kensler home, seven people were inside the house, rummaging around. What might have been evidence had already been trampled under.

To add to the difficultly of the case, Michigan State Police Crime Laboratory technicians were called to the scene, but the call was canceled by a high-ranking officer in the sheriff's department.

Police did find four shotgun shells at the site. The house had not been ransacked, and Kensler's wallet was found on his bed.

Among those at the scene was Robert Kensler, the brother of Peter, who described his brother as friendly and outgoing. Robert discounted the proxy fight at the bank as a motive for the murder, saying, "It may be more personal." He added that his brother "had one enemy." Robert did not elaborate on these statements—at least not to reporters.

Peter Kensler did have at least one enemy. The year before the murder, someone had fired a high-powered rifle through a window of his house. Kensler was not home at the time. No one was arrested for the act, but Kensler may have known who did it. There had also been a break-in at the house the year before the shooting. Nothing was stolen. As a result of the break-in, Kensler had an alarm installed at the house.

Detectives soon eliminated robbery as a motive for the murder, as there were many valuable items in the house and none of these were missing. His personal papers appeared to have been left undisturbed.

As the investigation progressed, detectives soon concluded that Kensler was murdered by someone he knew and was the sole target of the killer.

About two weeks after the murder, Jackson County sheriff's deputies found two boxes of 20-gage shotgun shells two or three miles from the Kensler home. These shells were the same number, brand and caliber as those found at the murder scene. Four shells were missing from one of the boxes. The shells were sent to the Michigan State Police Crime Lab at Lansing, but the results failed to offer any new clues.

By the end of June 1976, detectives had interviewed some seventy people, including family members and friends of Kensler. "They've been helpful and cooperative," said Lieutenant Laird Harris of the sheriff's department to the *Ann Arbor News* on March 8, 1976, "but you would think they would know more than they actually do about Kensler. There doesn't seem to be one person who can put it all together for us now….Kensler," said Harris, "was a more complicated man than anyone realized. We have a complex character living a complex life."

Detectives who were searching for a motive looked into the business dealings of Kensler and found some of them to be "questionable." Kensler, it was discovered, had at least two identities that he used for out-of-town meetings. It is not clear why Kensler felt the need to use false identities.

Kensler, it seems, had told people in the weeks before the murder that a prominent Manchester resident had threatened his life. He further stated that he was being followed and had confronted the man.

Detectives were told that Kensler had a folder of business documents that he said contained evidence against his enemies. This folder, it was said, was carried by Kensler at all times. This folder has never been found.

When the investigation began, six detectives were assigned to the case to interview family members, friends and business associates of Kensler. By the end of June, there were only two detectives. "Look," explained a detective to the *Ann Arbor News* on June 27, 1976, "this is a completed case. There are some things we have questions for and other things for which we have answers but no questions."

After nine months of investigating, detectives had narrowed down their list of suspects to one man, a downriver resident who had known Kensler for ten years. When questioned by detectives, the man, on advice of legal counsel, proved to be uncooperative. There was not enough evidence to seek a warrant. The investigation had come to an end.

There was no one else to question or any new leads to follow. There were other crimes that needed to be investigated. The Kensler case was placed on the back burner to be reopened should new evidence be uncovered.

Possible new evidence might have come to the surface in April 1982, six years after the murder. An anonymous caller told officers at the Jackson State Police Post "that the river has many secrets." The caller directed the officers to a site on Sharon Valley Road, where it crosses the River Raisin, about two miles from where Kensler had lived. At the site, state police divers recovered some twenty-seven items, "including drills, circular saws, radio equipment, a chain saw engine, red tire balancer with weights and an air impact wrench," according to the *Ann Arbor News* from April 15, 1982.

On the last dive, the diver probed the mud from which the items had been recovered. From the mud, the diver recovered a corroded 20-gauge pump shotgun, the same type of weapon used to kill Kensler. The shotgun had clearly been in the river far longer than the other items recovered. Upon examination of the weapon, it was found that the serial numbers had been ground off. Tests on the weapon could not prove that it was the weapon used to kill Kensler, but they did not rule it out either. "While we had no success in identifying it as the murder weapon," said lieutenant David Balasch, the head of the firearms section of the State Police Crime Lab in Northville, to the *Ann Arbor News* on April 28, 1982, "we couldn't positively eliminate it either. Make it a 50–50 statement….My partner 'raised' some partial parts numbers, but we don't yet have a serial number sufficient to trace the weapon." Detective William Mulholland, who was then in charge of the investigation, added, "This leaves us right where we were before the gun was found."

The murder of Peter Kensler remains unsolved.

15

MISSING PERSON

THE CASE OF KRISTINE KURTZ

Kristine Kurtz lived alone on her 113-acre farm near Independence Lake, north of Ann Arbor in Webster Township. She told friends she felt safe there. On Saturday, November 24, 1990, Craig Woods stopped by the farm and talked with Kurtz about the Detroit Lions beating the Denver Broncos that Thanksgiving. They talked about an addition Kurtz wanted Woods to build for her. The two also completed a financial transaction. Then Woods left the farm at dinner time, and Kurtz returned to the house to watch horse racing on television, her 6:30 p.m. ritual.

Another friend, Teresa Helle, called Kurtz on Sunday, but the call went unanswered. This was not unusual, as Kurtz cared for her animals and often did not answer the phone. That same day, Helle stopped by the house to drop off food she had prepared for Kurtz. She saw that the dogs were in the house and that Kurtz's truck was gone. Helle called Kurtz again on Monday and on Tuesday during *Family Feud*, which Kurtz always watched. Once again, the call went unanswered. That day, Helle went to the house and found the dogs still in the house and the horses still in the barn. Kurtz always let the horses out first thing in the morning.

Friends knew Kurtz was not the type of person to just go away and leave her animals unattended. Her pets included Voodoo the cat, Clover the goat, Knuckles the boxer dog and Zipper the fox terrier, as well as eleven Arabian horses, each with its own name. When she did leave on a trip, she would arrange for someone to look after her pets and horses. Then she would call every other day or so to check in.

Once police were informed of Kurtz's disappearance, they began a search of the property. A helicopter from the Michigan State Police equipped with an infrared camera to detect heat from a human body searched the farm from the air. A ground search with dogs was carried on the farm out as well. Because Kurtz's truck was missing, police searched the trails and the road around the farm in case she had driven the truck off the road and was trapped in a ditch. The searches found no trace of Kurtz.

The police carried out the investigation as a possible abduction. There was reason for concern.

There had been as many as twenty burglaries in Webster Township starting in September and continuing until Thanksgiving. Some of these burglaries had occurred near where Kurtz lived. Suspicion had fallen on twenty-eight-year-old Bernard Edward Brooks, who was last seen on the day Kurtz disappeared.

There was no evidence linking Brooks to the disappearance of Kurtz, but the investigation was conducted due to the possibility that the two cases were linked. The police had no evidence that a crime had even been committed. Rain had fallen in the days after Kurtz was last seen alive and before the investigation in the days after Kurtz was last seen alive. Evidence might have been washed away by the rain. Police thought several items might be missing from the home, including a television, a VCR and a radio. Police could not be sure, as the house, like the animals, were being looked after by several friends. There was an added reason for concern: In some of the burglaries, guns were among the items stolen. Brooks was considered armed and dangerous.

The family of Kurtz offed a reward of $25,000 for information that led to the safe return of Kurtz. Now all that family and friends could do was await developments and hope for the best.

Kristine Kurtz was born on December 2, 1949, in Detroit, Michigan, the daughter of Richard J. and Mary Ellen Kurtz. Her father owned a steel company in Detroit and was well-off. He and his wife died in a private plane crash in 1957, and Kristine and her older sister and brother were raised by an aunt in Grosse Point. Their grandfather set up a trust fund for the children. Their aunt kept a careful watch on the fund for the benefit of the children.

By the late 1960s, Kristine had dropped out of Eastern Michigan University and was managing a small boutique called Stangers on West

Cross Street in Ypsilanti. Not yet twenty-one years old, she did not have access to the trust fund and worked to earn enough to get by. At the time, she was living with Gregory Fournier in an apartment on College Place.

On the evening of June 30, 1968, Kristine and Gregory went out to visit friends. On the way home, they stopped in Abby's Party Store on the corner of Ballard and West Cross Streets. There, they purchased a bag of groceries. The two left the store and walked a block up Ballard Street and turned right onto Emmett Street, toward College Place. As they walked down Emmett Street, a car pulled up beside them. It was a warm, muggy evening, so the windows of the car were rolled down. Kristine and Gregory could see that there were three men in the car. The driver called out to Kristine, "Hey, baby. Want to go out with some real men?"

"Hey man," replied Gregory. "She's with me."

To this, the driver shouted, "Shut the fuck up, asshole, or the three of us will get out and kick the shit out of you."

Then Kristine expressed her opinion: "What a bunch of dickless wonders! Three against one, you cowardly faggots!"

Surprised by her response, the driver hit the gas pedal and left the couple in a cloud of screeching tires and stinking exhaust.

This occurred just after 9:00 p.m.

That same evening, around 10:30 p.m., Joan Schell, a twenty-year-old student at Eastern Michigan University, was standing in front of McKenny Union on Cross Street. She was desperate to see her boyfriend in Ann Arbor and, having missed the last bus to Ann Arbor, had resorted to hitchhiking. Soon after, a car pulled up with three young men inside. Schell accepted the offer for a ride to Ann Arbor and got in the car. This was the last time anyone saw Joan Schell alive. The body of Joan Schell was found on the roadside in Ann Arbor Township on July 5, 1968. She is considered the second victim of serial killer John Norman Collins, known as the Co-Ed Killer.

Gregory Fournier believes it was Collins who was driving the car when the three men tried to pick up Kristine Kurtz.

In time, Kristine and Gregory went their separate ways. Kristine was later married, and she and her husband planned to build a home in Webster Township. Then, after a few years, the couple was divorced. At the age of thirty, Kristine began to receive funds from her trust. This was not a large fund, but because of her needs, she was able to live off the interest. Her largest expenses included food, hay and dog food.

The *Ann Arbor News* reported on December 9, 1990:

According to friends and family, Kurtz spends most of her time caring for her animals, reading, working on arts and crafts projects—most of them, this year's Christmas gifts—and watching sports on television.

Back issues of National Geographic, International Wildlife *and* Equus *magazines are stacked in her house. Books about homes, such as* More Great American Mansions *and* American Bungalow, 1800–1930, *fill book stands. Some one hundred videotapes of horse races and rodeos—zapped from a satellite dish—are crammed into a bookcase.*

Boxes of jigsaw puzzles are scattered on the floor. Large stuffed animals—a frog, giraffe, ostrich and lion—sit on a couch. A half-completed hat rack, designed in the shape of a moose, covers a table. On an easel, an acrylic painting is almost done—the scene copied from a postcard portraying cows in a pasture.

Friends continued to care for Kurtz's animals in the hopes that she would return. Some sought the help of psychics, one of whom said Kristine would be found in a few days. As the days passed, the hope began to fade.

On the day after Christmas 1990, Rick Godfrey was in the barn counting bales of hay so he could order more. As he did, he spotted a pair of boots under the bales. He recognized the pair as those he had given to Kristine as a birthday present three years before. He moved a bale of hay and uncovered a body. The bales had been arranged around the body like a coffin. Godfrey called the police, who spent seven hours gathering evidence before removing the body. The body was not immediately identified as that of Kristine Kurtz, as it was frozen, decomposition had set in and cats had eaten some of the remains. Dental records proved the body was that of Kurtz, and the autopsy determined she had died of a gunshot wound.

Brooks was taken into custody by police at the home of his parents in Saucier, Mississippi, around 12:30 a.m., on December 31, 1990. The Harrison County Sheriff's Department had received a teletype from the Colorado probation department informing them that a warrant for Brooks's arrest had been issued on November 20, 1990. This was for violation of probation in connection with an attempted theft. The teletype was sent on December 28, 1990, as it was considered likely Brooks would return home to visit his family.

After his arrest, Brooks led police to the parking lot of a nearby apartment complex, where he had parked Kurtz's 1987 Ford truck. Police searched the truck and found several items that proved to have been stolen.

Brooks was arraigned that morning on a charge of possession of cocaine, which had been found on his person at the time of his arrest. No bond was set due to the warrant for parole violation in Colorado. The Michigan State Police had issued a warrant for his arrest in connection with the burglaries in Webster Township. Brooks was returned to Michigan on February 7, 1991, and faced arraignment on a charge of murder, as well as four counts of burglary, the next day.

Those who knew Bernard Brooks said he was a nice guy with a record of nonviolent crime. For a time, Brooks had lived in Colorado and Virginia, and in each state, he left a record of embezzlement and forged checks. Then in late 1989, he moved to Washtenaw County. In September 1990, he left his wife and stayed in numerous area hotels. Later that month, a string of burglaries began in Webster Township. Among the items stolen were guns, jewelry and food.

On October 15, 1990, hunters found stolen property in an abandoned silo. Among the items were personal papers, which linked Brooks to the stolen property. An arrest warrant was issued for Brooks on a charge of burglary and concealing stolen property. "A month later, November 20, Brooks was spotted riding a mountain bicycle on North Territorial Road, near Jennings Road. Northfield Township police chief John Shosey tried to apprehend Brooks, but he jumped into the woods and fled. State police dogs couldn't find him," reported the *Ann Arbor News* on December 9, 1990. Brooks had dropped a field jacket, from which police recovered a loaded handgun and binoculars, which, like the jacket, had been stolen in Webster Township.

The trial of Bernard Brooks began on Tuesday, August 6, 1991, with the impaneling of a jury of eight women and four men. The trial opened with Brooks pleading guilty to two charges of breaking and entering two homes in Webster Township. He denied committing the murder of Kurtz.

In his opening statement, Prosecutor Lynwood Noah told the jury that Bernard Brooks had shot and killed Kristine Kurtz during the commission of a burglary. He added that Brooks and Kurtz had met "in a fatal collision." Assistant Public Defender Walter White said, "They were more like ships passing in the night. They were in the same place at the same time, but they never met."

Prosecutor Lynwood Noah had to build his case on a string of circumstantial evidence from the burglaries Brooks had confessed to. There were no eyewitnesses to the murder, and the murder weapon had never been found.

Sometime on the night of October 12, 1990, testified Kenneth R. Kingsbury of Webster Township, someone had stolen a .357 Magnum from his home. A bowling bag, food and liquor were stolen as well.

On the evening of October 23, 1990, Katherine and Stephen Salant of Ann Arbor were confronted by Brooks, they testified, who brandished the .357 Magnum that had been stolen from the Kingsbury home. The gun was found a block away from the Salant home.

Webster Township resident William Miller testified that on November 14, 1990, a burglar had taken his .38-caliber Smith and Wesson revolver, as well as a gunbelt containing twenty-five rounds of .38-caliber Lubaloy shells. A .38-caliber Special Winchester Lubaloy bullet had been removed from the body of Kurtz during an autopsy. This type of bullet had not been manufactured since 1975.

Hubert Lintz of Webster Township told the court that on November 17, 1990, a burglar had stolen a 9-millimeter semiautomatic, .22-caliber Browning target pistol and a .38-caliber Colt Diamondback Special revolver, which was in a distinctive brown vinyl case.

Brooks had confessed to each of the burglaries but told detectives during questioning that he had not stolen the Colt Diamondback revolver that belonged to Lintz. This was the weapon detectives believed he used to kill Kurtz. This weapon had never been recovered. Detectives did find the revolver that belonged to Lintz in Kurtz's truck after Brooks was arrested. The revolver was in the brown case that had been stolen from the Miller home.

"Oakland County medical examiner Lyubisa Dragovic testified that Kurtz was killed by a single gunshot that entered her upper-left back and passed through her left lung, aorta, heart and right lung before lodging in her right breast," reported the *Ann Arbor News* on August 8, 1991. The fatal shot had been fired at close range.

Michigan State Police firearms expert Jon Stanton testified that Kurtz was killed by either a .38- or a .357-caliber Lubaloy bullet with six ridges and grooves with a left-hand-twice. Public Defender White pointed out that twenty-five Lubaloy bullets had been found in the search of Kurtz's truck. Prosecutor White noted that there may have been more of these bullets stolen than stated in testimony.

The defense called only one witness, Bernard Brooks, who told the court about living out of a ranger's booth in Independence Lake Park after losing his job and wife. He made a living by stealing food, liquor, warm clothes and valuables. "He said he found and stole a half pound of cocaine and a quantity of marijuana from Kurtz's isolated farmhouse, as well as piles of twenty-dollar bills left on a dresser, a radio, television and VCR, but never saw a trace of the woman," reported the *Ann Arbor News* on August 8, 1991.

Prosecutor Noah told the jury that Brooks could have stolen the cocaine from one of his other burglaries and reminded them that Kurtz lived off a trust fund worth about $1 million. She had no need, as the defense argued, to sell cocaine to support herself.

The case was turned over to the jury, and after five hours of deliberation, they returned a verdict of guilty of murder in the first degree. This meant a sentence of life in prison for Brooks.

At the sentencing, Defense Attorney White asked visiting Judge Thomas Roumell to set aside the verdict of the jury. He said a pretrial ruling by Judge Ross Campbell had damaged Brooks's right to a fair trial. Judge Campbell had stepped down from the case due to illness. The autopsy had revealed that Kurtz had cocaine in her bloodstream at the time of her death. Judge Campbell had ruled to exclude this evidence, as, he said, this would have no relevance other than character assassination. The defense had wished to present the possibility that Kurtz had been murdered as the result of a drug deal gone bad, but they could not advance this argument because of the ruling. Judge Roumell said, "I'm aware of the appropriateness of your motion, but I'm in complete and full agreement with Judge Campbell's rulings....Had the court been trying the case instead of the jury, it would have reached the same inescapable and unavoidable conclusion of guilt."

Judge Roumell passed a sentence of life imprisonment on Brooks.

The case was sent to the Michigan State Court of Appeals, which affirmed the lower court.

The case was then sent to the Michigan State Supreme Court, which, in December 1996, overturned the conviction and ordered the case be retried. "The fact that Ms. Kurtz had cocaine in her bloodstream does not prove that she was killed by a drug dealer, nor does it prove anything else," ruled the court. "However, it is a piece of evidence that was relevant to the defense that the defendant sought to present."

The new trial was set to begin in December 1998. Public Defender Ronald Q. Brown received information that had not been made available to the defense before the first trial. "That information included a Michigan State Police surveillance of [Betty Ann] Chiavarini, a federal Drug Enforcement Administration report on Chiavarini's drug trafficking and police information on the drug activities of Chiavarini, Kurtz and

George Craig Wood, the last known person to see Kurtz alive," reported the *Ann Arbor News* on November 26, 1998.

Betty Ann Chiavarini, a friend of Kurtz, had been convicted on drug charges in 1991 but failed to show up for sentencing and fled to Florida. Chiavarini had inherited half of Kurtz's $1 million estate.

"Besides the new police information," the account from the *Ann Arbor News* continued, "Brown said he received two anonymous letters providing such details as what Kurtz's friends did—such as getting rid of cocaine and scales left out in Kurtz's kitchen—while she was missing. The writer also suspected that someone Kurtz knew—and not Brooks—killed her."

Assistant Prosecutor Eric Gutenberg called the letter "a piece of fiction." He suggested it was the work of a friend of Brooks who wrote it on his behalf.

Chiavarini was located and returned to Michigan but invoked her Fifth Amendment right against self-incrimination.

George Craig Wood testified on the second day of the trial that he had been in a "friendly, platonic relationship" with Kurtz. He admitted that on November 24, 1990, he purchased one-eighth of an ounce of cocaine from Kurtz for $200. Woods admitted he had purchased cocaine from Kurtz two or three times a week for the two years leading up to her death. When asked why he did not tell the police about the transaction at the time of her disappearance, he explained, "I believed that Kurtz was still alive, and I didn't want to see her get in trouble, and I didn't want to get in trouble....I wanted the opportunity to tell the truth to the jury. I believe it's a way for me to cleanse myself of my past life. I do regret that the truth did not come out."

Brooks again took the stand in his defense and denied killing Kurtz.

At the end of the trial, the jury, after thirteen hours of deliberation, was unable to agree on a verdict, and a new trial was scheduled.

Before the third trial could start, the prosecutor's office offered Brooks a plea bargain. He could enter a plea of no contest to a charge of second-degree murder, which carried the maximum penalty of life in prison but with the possibility of parole. Instead of running the risk of a trial, Brooks accepted the offer.

On May 5, 2000, Brooks was sentenced to twenty to thirty years in prison, with credit for the 3,414 days already served.

At the hearing, Kathleen Kurtz, a sister of Kristine, addressed Brooks: "I hope, Mr. Brooks, that you take this time to think about what your goals are...how you can better your life and make some meaning out of your life for you, your family, society as a whole.…I hope by the time you are paroled that you will have managed to find something to do…that does not involve break-ins, murder…something that will be better for all of us." Then she turned to Brooks family, "I apologize to [the Brooks] family that this had to happen to all of us."

BIBLIOGRAPHY

A Terrible Affair at Lyndon: The Murder of Martin Breitenbach

Chapman, Charles C. *History of Washtenaw County, Michigan*. Chicago: Chas. C. & Co., 1881.

Michigan Argus. "Murder Near Chelsea." August 8, 1873.

Peninsular Courier. "The Lyndon Tragedy." August 8, 1873.

Ypsilanti Commercial. August 9, 1873.

Murdered in His Own Bed: The Death of Ludwig Miller

Beaks, Samuel W. *Past and Present of Washtenaw County, Michigan*. Chicago: S.J. Clarke Publishing Co., 1906.

Chapman, Charles C. *History of Washtenaw County, Michigan*. Chicago: Chas. C. & Co., 1881.

Detroit Evening News. "The Boy Murderer." September 22, 1875

———. "The Scio Murder." August 12, 1875.

———. "Tragedy Near Dexter." August 11, 1875.

Michigan Argus. "Burkhardt at the Prison." October 1, 1875.

———. "Horrible Crime at Scio." April 13, 1875.

———. "Sentence of Burkhardt." September 24, 1875.

Peninsular Courier. "Burkhardt, the Boy Murderer." August 21, 1875.

———. "Murder!" August 13, 1875.

Murder at Dexter

Ann Arbor Courier. "Dexter Murder." January 25, 1878.

Chapman, Charles C. *History of Washtenaw County, Michigan.* Chicago: Chas. C. & Co., 1881.

Evening News. "A Murderous Hermit." January 21, 1878.

The Linsley Shooting in Bridgewater

Ann Arbor Courier. "Bridgewater Furnishes a Horrible Tragedy." April 17, 1889.

———. "David Lindley Had a Hearing." April 24, 1889.

Ann Arbor Democrat. "A Distressing Affair." April 19, 1889.

Detroit Evening News. "A Father Kills His Son." April 15, 1889.

Detroit Free Press. "The Linsley Shooting." April 16, 1889.

Bank Robbery at Dexter

Ann Arbor Register. "A Bold Bank Robbery." March 1, 1894.

———. "Gregory, An Imbecile." March 15, 1894.

Detroit Free Press. "Bold Bank Robbery." March 2, 1894.

———. "The Mystery Is Solved." March 7, 1894.

Evening News. "Detroit, Desperate." March 1, 1894.

———. "Double Job." March 2, 1894.

———. "He Did It." March 6, 1894.

Washtenaw Evening Times. "Is Still a Mystery." March 2, 1894.

———. "The Money Is Found." March 6, 1894.

———. "They Did a Slick Job." March 1, 1894.

———. "Where Credit Is Due." March 7, 1894.

Ypsilanti Commercial. "Gregory Confessed." March 9, 1894.

"They Shined Me": The Murder of James Richards

Ann Arbor Argus. "Are They the Men?" February 19, 1897.

———. "Formally Arraigned." February 18, 1897.

———. "Had Their Hearing." March 12, 1897.

————. "Has Counsel Much Talk." March 19, 1897.

————. "James Richards's Property." March 19, 1897.

————. "Shot Down." February 5, 1897.

————. "A Very Peculiar Dream." March 15, 1897.

Ann Arbor Register. "Are They Guilty?" March 11, 1897.

————. "A Bold Robbery in Superior." August 18, 1880.

————. "Gone a Glemmering." November 4, 1897.

————. "The James Richards Estate." March 18, 1897.

————. "James Richards's Money." March 24, 1897.

————. "Long and Tedious." October 28, 1897.

————. "Mrs. Straub Talks." March 24, 1897.

————. "Murdered." February 4, 1897.

————. "New Evidence Found." March 4, 1897.

————. "Serious." February 18, 1897.

————. "Who Killed Richards?" October 14, 1897.

Beaks, Samuel W. *Past and Present of Washtenaw County, Michigan*. Chicago: S.J. Clarke Publishing Co., 1906.

Detroit Free Press. "Detroit, Bold Robbery Near Ann Arbor." August 14, 1880.

————. "Has Fairly Started." February 20, 1897.

————. "Left Him to Die Alone." February 2, 1897.

————. "Richards Murder Trial." October 20, 1897.

————. "Richards Murder Trial." October 23, 1897.

————. "Richards Murder Trial." October 24, 1897.

Washtenaw Evening Times. "Attorneys Talking." October 28, 1897.

————. "The Chief Witness." October 23, 1897.

————. "The Defense Opens." October 26, 1897.

————. "Evidence Is All In." October 27, 1897.

————. "Important Evidence." October 21, 1897.

————. "Judson's Testimony." October 26, 1897.

————. "Jury Takes a Trip." October 25, 1897.

————. "The Richards Trial." October 20, 1897.

————. "Talk of Tracks." October 21, 1897.

————. "Their Stories Agree." October 23, 1897.

————. "They Are Free Men." October 29, 1897.

————. "They Know the Men." October 22, 1897.

————. "They Near the End." October 22, 1897.

————. "Will the Alibi Stand." October 27, 1897.

William, Karl. "The Murder of James Richards in Superior Township." Unpublished paper, 1997. Reprinted, 2010.

Ypsilanti Commercial. "Crime Report." February 5, 1897.
———. "Examination of the Three." March 12, 1897.
———. "Marshal Paterson." March 5, 1897.
Ypsilantian. "Murder Near Dixboro." February 4, 1897.

Death of an Unkind Father

Daily Times News. "Jealous Angers Man Ends Life." January 3, 1910.
Ypsilanti Daily Press. "Unkind Father Suicides After a Long Spree." January 3, 1910.

Death at the Depot

Ann Arbor Daily Times News. "Ann Arbor, Robbers in Gun Duel." January 7, 1910.
———. "Bullet with Steel Jacket Killed Him." January 8, 1910.
———. "Plead Guilty to the Charge: Bound Over." January 10, 1910.
Detroit Free Press. "Captured, Shot." January 8, 1910.
Detroit News. "Young Bandits in Death Fight in Ypsilanti." January 7, 1910.
Ypsilanti Daily Press. "All Theories Shattered by Kind of Bullet." January 10, 1910.
———. "Emmett Affirms the *Daily Press* Theory." January 21, 1910.
———. "Emmett Is Alive, Boy Bandit Sign Guilt Confession." January 8, 1910.
———. "Gun Men Slay in Bloody Fight." January 7, 1910.
———. "Harrington Murderer of Henry Miner." February 8, 1910.
———. "Harrington's Preliminary Examination." February 7, 1910.
———. "Harrington Tried This Afternoon." March 8, 1910.
———. "Harrington Will Not Be Arraigned Now." February 2, 1910.
———. "McCormick Gets Life, Billings 5 to 10 Years." January 11, 1910.
———. "M'Cormick and Pal Are Captured." March 8, 1910.
———. "M'Cormick, the Boy Bandit, Breaks Prison," March 7, 1910.
———. "Prosecutor Carl Storm Gives Statement." January 22, 1910.
———. "Reformatory Crime School, Says McCormick." January 12, 1910.
———. "Rhea Talks Tel. Operator Hears Shots." January 8, 1910.
———. "Young Outlaw Who Robbed Ypsi Store Dies at Jackson." September 6, 1910.

Whittaker Jewelry Store Robbery

Ann Arbor Times News. "Aged Whittaker Man Is Rolled." October 31, 1921.
———. "Two Are Held in Whittaker Robbery Case." November 1, 1921.
Daily Ypsilanti Press. "Gets 12 to 24 Years Sentence." April 13, 1922.
———. "Have Hard Time Getting Jury to Try Stanch." March 8, 1922.
———. "Lawyer Halts Stanch Case." March 10, 1922.
———. "Select Jury to Try Stanch for Jewel Robbery." March 7, 1922.
———. "Stanch Found Guilty." March 18, 1922.
———. "Stanch Hopes to Establish Strong Alibi." March 14, 1922.
———. "Stanch Jury Is Still Debating Prisoner's Fate." March 17, 1922.
———. "Stanch Jury Still Out, Given Case Yesterday." March 16, 1922.
———. "Two Arrests in Whittaker Store Robbery." November 1, 1921.
———. "Whittaker Jeweler Rolled by Bandits." October 31, 1921.
Ypsilanti Record. "Jury Brings in Verdict Guilty." March 23, 1922.
———. "Stanch Fate in Hands of Jury." March 16, 1922.
———. "Stanch Jury Out 20 Hours." December 15, 1921.
———. "Whittaker Man Robbed $2,000." November 2, 1921.

A Lonely Grave for Harry Cyb

Victor, Bate J. "Snaring Michigan's Hammer Slayers." N.p., n.d.
Washtenaw Tribune. "Cyb Murder Nears Solution." March 2, 1931.
———. "Two Cyb Murders Get Life." March 4, 1931.
Ypsilanti Daily Press. "Arrival of State Officer Delayed Case Marks Time." February 5, 1926.
———. "Attorneys Summoned for Cyb Trial March 8." February 27, 1926.
———. "Bail Denied Men Accused of Cyb Crime by Curtiss." September 29, 1925.
———. "Crossies, Lidke Take Stand in Own Defense." March 17, 1926.
———. "Cyb Case Awaits Action by State, February Ordered to Start Cyb Case." February 18, 1926.
———. "Cyb Case Is Resumed Here this Afternoon." October 3, 1925.
———. "Cyb Case Waits State Decision Expected Soon." February 6, 1926.
———. "Cyb Case Will Start Monday." January 19, 1926.
———. "Cyb Slayers Given Life Sentences Today." March 3, 1931.
———. "Cyb Slaying Facts to Be Probed by State." February 3, 1926.
———. "Cyb Suspects to Await Next Term." November 16, 1925.

——. "Evidence Insufficient Prosecutor's Opinion." February 13, 1926.

——. "Examination in Cyb Slaying Case Starts." October 2, 1925.

——. "Four Jurymen Excused as Cyb Trial Starts." March 9, 1926.

——. "Herman Crossie Not Guilty." March 20, 1926.

——. "Jury May Get Crossie Case this Afternoon." March 10, 1926.

——. "Jury to Determine Guilt of Crossies, Owen Lidke." February 12, 1926.

——. "Jury to Hear Herman Crossie's Story Next." March 18, 1926.

——. "Laird to Prosecute Cyb Case." February 16, 1926.

——. "Owen Lidke Obtains Bail, Crossie Fails." October 8, 1925.

——. "Preparations Start for Trying Cyb Case." February 20, 1926.

——. "Slaying Mystery for Over Five Years, Solved by Confession." February 28, 1931.

——. "State May Press Cyb Trial." February 1, 1926.

——. "State Not to Prosecute in Cyb Case." February 8, 1926.

——. "State Promises Action in Cyb Case, Three Courses Considered." February 2, 1926.

——. "State to Investigate Cyb Slaying Further." February 15, 1926.

——. "Terry Sentence in Cyb Case Deferred." March 2, 1931.

——. "Willis Man Brutally Slain, Police Hold Three Suspects." September 21, 1925.

New York Officer Shot

Ann Arbor Daily News. "Tourist Shot in Plymouth Road Holdup." September 18, 1930.

Detroit Free Press. "Scorned Loot to Kill, Theory." September 18, 1930.

Detroit Times. "Admits Raid on Jail, May Get Life." October 30, 1930.

——. "Asked to Name Pal as Killer." October 17, 1930.

——. "Bandit's Wife 18, Life 1 of 4 Held in Jail Plot." October 28, 1930.

——. "Boy Gets Life Day After Killing." October 12, 1930.

——. "Detective Blinded by Mystery Gunmen." September 18, 1930.

——. "Detroit Trio Accused in Ann Arbor." October 29, 1930.

——. "Girl, 18, Freed in Jail Plot." October 31, 1930.

——. "Hunt Officer's Assailants." September 19, 1930.

——. "Jail 4 in Shooting of N.Y. Policeman." September 21, 1930.

——. "Life for Aide in Jail Plot." November 4, 1930.

————. "Mountjoy, M., W., Her First Real Sweetheart Sent to Prison as Killer." October 12, 1930.

————. "Quiz Detroiter in Shooting." October 15, 1930.

————. "Renew Search for Gunmen." September 22, 1930.

————. "Youth Kill Policeman, Crows Threatens Jail." October 11, 1930.

New York Times. "Peter J. O'Rourke, Obituary." March 13, 1954.

Ypsilanti Daily Press. "Brown Suspects Maintain Silence." October 29, 1930.

————. "Confession of Brown Unknown to Prosecutor." October 18, 1930.

————. "Dailey Identifies Man Who Sought Brow's Release." October 28, 1930.

————. "Deputies Patrol Roads Following Wanton Shooting." September 19, 1930.

————. "Deputy Frustrates Jail Break, Brown Sentenced to Life Term." October 27, 1930.

————. "Four Suspects Held Today for O'Rourke Attack." September 20, 1930.

————. "Life Term Given M'Comis, Brown to Be Returned." October 13, 1930.

————. "New York Officer Shot on Plymouth Road." September 18, 1930.

————. "Pyle and Brown Sign Confessions Involving Sister." October 30, 1930.

————. "Sister of Brown to Be Arraigned Today, Sample Remains Ill." October 31, 1930.

————. "Suspects Freed in O'Rourke Case." September 23, 1930.

————. "Thugs Who Shot O'Rourke Known." October 1, 1930.

————. "Tony Pyle Given Life for Effort to Free Gunman." November 2, 1930.

————. "Two Suspects in O'Rourke Case in Jail in Pt. Huron." October 11, 1930.

McHenry Killings

Ann Arbor News. "Local Girl Kills Mother, Brother, Self." October 1, 1937.

————. "Same Gun Used in Double Murder and Girl's Suicide." October 2, 1937.

Detroit Free Press. "Daughter Kills Two, Ends Life." October 2, 1937.

Detroit News. "Brooding Girl Turns Slayer." October 2, 1937.

————. "McHenry Family Holds Triple Rites." October 4, 1937.

————. "She Knew Not What She Did." October 3, 1937.

————. "Woman and Boy Found Slain in Car After Girl Kills Self." October 1, 1937.

Detroit Times. "Co-ed Kills Mother, Brother; Shoots 2nd Boy, Ends Own Life." October 1, 1937.

————. "Girl's Gun Mystifies Police." October 1, 1937.

————. "Girl's Killer Ruse to Get Gun Revealed by Her Father." October 2, 1937.

————. "Withhold Rites in Triple Deaths for Police Probe." October 3, 1937.

Ypsilanti Daily Press. "Girl Shoots Mother, 2 Brothers, Kills Self." October 1, 1937.

————. "Officers Checking Identity of Killer in McHenry Deaths." October 2, 1937.

————. "Rites Held for McHenry Victims." October 5, 1937.

Eleanor Farver Murder:
The Search for the Man Who Did Not Exist

Ann Arbor News. "Aid Asked in Suspect Hunt." September 25, 1970.

————. "Fugitive's Letter Revealed." November 13, 1970.

————. "Search Continues for Suspect." September 24, 1970.

————. "Suspect Believed Hiding Near Home." October 11, 1970.

Barton, John. "He Had a Name till He Murdered; Then He Turned Out to Be Nobody." *Ann Arbor News*, June 20, 1983.

Cackley, Phil. "Burns Guilty of 2nd-Degree Murder." *Ypsilanti Press*, December 4, 1987.

————. "Burns: Shooting Death Accidental." *Ypsilanti Press*, December 1, 1987.

————. "Burns Shotgun Slaying Trial to Begin." *Ypsilanti Press*, November 23, 1987.

————. "Fugitive Admits to Murder of Lover; Faces Prelim Exam." *Ypsilanti Press*, June 3, 1987.

————. "Prosecution Rests Case Against Burns." *Ypsilanti Press*, November 27, 1987.

————. "Shotgun Killing Accidental—Attorney." *Ypsilanti Press*, November 25, 1987.

———. "Testimony Begins in Burns Trial." *Ypsilanti Press*, August 18, 1987.

———. "Testimony Ends in Burns Murder Trial." *Ypsilanti Press*, December 3, 1987.

Heppe, Linda. "17-Year Search Suspect Ends in Penn." *Ypsilanti Press*, June 1, 1987.

Oppat, Susan. "Arraignment Set in Slaying." *Ann Arbor News*, June 2, 1987.

———. "Extradition Hearing Set in 1970 Murder Case." *Ann Arbor News*, June 1, 1987.

———. "'Old and Tired' Suspect Arraigned." *Ann Arbor News*, June 3, 1987.

———. "17-Year-Old Murder Case to Be Tried." *Ann Arbor News*, August 18, 1987.

———. "TV Leads to Killer." *Ann Arbor News*, May 31, 1987.

Reynolds, Roy. "Cashman Guilty in Lover's Murder." *Ann Arbor News*, December 4, 1987.

———. "Defendant in Murder May Testify Today." *Ann Arbor News*, November 25, 1987.

———. "Re-enactment." *Ann Arbor News*, December 3, 1987.

———. "Suspect: 'I Didn't Kill Her. The Gun Shot Her. I Didn't.'" *Ann Arbor News*, December 1, 1987.

———. "Unsigned Evidence: 'I Shot and Killed the Woman I Loved.'" *Ann Arbor News*, November 26, 1987.

Treml, William. "Killer Dies Before Sentencing." *Ann Arbor News*, January 8, 1988.

———. "Woman Slain; Man Is Hunted." *Ann Arbor News*, September 23, 1970.

Kensler Murder at Manchester

Ann Arbor News. "For the Record." March 13, 1976.

———. "Gun Found in River Raisin Suspected Murder Weapon." April 18, 1982.

———. "New Leads Found in Attorney's Death." February 16, 1976.

———. "No Prime Suspect in Lawyer Slaying." February 6, 1976.

———. "Physical Evidence Found in Slaying." February 17, 1976.

———. "Shotgun Can't Be Linked to Murder." April 18, 1982.

———. "Slaying Probe Continues." February 7, 1976.

Barton, John. "Kensler Murder Stumps Police Investigators." *Ann Arbor News*, June 27, 1976.

Kane, Jim. "Manchester Attorney Found Slain." *Ann Arbor News*, February 5, 1976.

Mcleister, Dan. "Business Disputes Marked Victim's Last Year." *Ann Arbor News*, February 5, 1976.

Oppat, Susan. "Detectives Sift Clues in 12-Year-Old Murder Case." *Ann Arbor News*, May 1, 1988.

Raphael, Steve. "Lawyer's Slaying Still a Mystery." *Ann Arbor News*, March 8, 1976.

Tremil, William. "Ex-President Sues Bank in Manchester." *Ann Arbor News*, March 11, 1976.

———. "Murder Washtenaw Style: Six Bizarre Cases and a Mystery." *Ann Arbor News*, February 5, 1985.

Missing Person: The Case of Kristine Kurtz

Ann Arbor News. "Court Overturns Conviction in Woman's Death." December 28, 1996.

———. "Obituaries, Kurtz, Kristine." December 29, 1990.

Cain, Stephen. "Brooks Says He Stole, Didn't Kill." *Ann Arbor News*, August 8, 1991.

———. "Cain, Murder Trial Hinges on Belt, Gun." *Ann Arbor News*, August 8, 1991.

Cobbs, Liz. "Closed Hearing Adds a New Twist to Trial." *Ann Arbor News*, December 5, 1998.

———. "Defense Seeks Missing Witness to Testify at Retrial of '90 Murder." *Ann Arbor News*, November 26, 1998.

———. "Man Pleads No Contest to Murder." *Ann Arbor News*, March 22, 2000.

———. "Murder Trial Enters 2nd Week." *Ann Arbor News*, December 8, 1998.

———. "Suspect Denies Killing Woman." *Ann Arbor News*, December 9, 1998.

———. "Victim Sold Drugs, Man Says." *Ann Arbor News*, December 2, 1998.

Eisenberg, Steve. "Authorities Seek Suspect's Return to State." *Ann Arbor News*, January 3, 1991.

———. "Bernard Brooks: A 'Nice Guy' Faces a Murder Charge." *Ann Arbor News*, February 17, 1991.

———. "Body May Be Missing Woman." *Ann Arbor News*, December 27, 1990.

———. "Brooks Ordered to Stand Trial in Kurtz Slaying." *Ann Arbor News*, February 21, 1991.

———. "Brooks, Suspect in Killing Arrested." *Ann Arbor News*, December 31, 1990.

———. "Mystery of Missing Woman Frustrates Friends, Police." *Ann Arbor News*, December 9, 1990.

Fournier, Gregory. "The Demise of Kristi Kurtz—November 1990." *Fornology*. www.fornology.com.

———. "Facing Down John Norman Collins—Kristi Kurtz." *Fornology*. www.fornology.com.

———. *Terror in Ypsilanti*. Tucson, AZ: Wheatmark, 2016.

Grantham, Russell. "Family of Woman Offers $25,000 Reward." *Ann Arbor News*, December 23, 1990.

Hugger, Mark. "Plea-Bargain Bid Fails in Webster Woman's Slaying" *Ypsilanti Press*, April 13, 1991.

———. "Trial Begins in Webster Slaying." *Ypsilanti Press*, August 7, 1991.

Oppat, Susan. "Brooks Gets Life Sentence in Fatal Shooting of Woman." *Ann Arbor News*, September 14, 1991.

———. "Man Pleads No Contest, Gets 20–30 Years for 1990 Death." *Ann Arbor News*, May 6, 2000.

Stewart, Will. "Police Check Possibility of Abduction in Woman's Disappearance." *Ann Arbor News*, December 1, 1990.

ABOUT THE AUTHOR

James Thomas Mann is a local historian in Ypsilanti, Michigan, and is the author of nine published books on local history. His works include *Wicked Washtenaw County*, *Wicked Ann Arbor* and *Wicked Ypsilanti*. He is also a frequent contributor to the *Ypsilanti Gleanings*, the publication of the Ypsilanti Historical Society. Mann is the host of the Highland Cemetery Lantern Tours every October.

Visit us at
www.historypress.com
···